C000154557

THIS IS YOUR **PASSBOOK**® FOR ...

SENIOR CLERK-STENOGRAPHER

NATIONAL LEARNING CORPORATION®
passbooks.com

PASSBOOK® SERIES

THE *PASSBOOK® SERIES* has been created to prepare applicants and candidates for the ultimate academic battlefield – the examination room.

At some time in our lives, each and every one of us may be required to take an examination – for validation, matriculation, admission, qualification, registration, certification, or licensure.

Based on the assumption that every applicant or candidate has met the basic formal educational standards, has taken the required number of courses, and read the necessary texts, the *PASSBOOK® SERIES* furnishes the one special preparation which may assure passing with confidence, instead of failing with insecurity. Examination questions – together with answers – are furnished as the basic vehicle for study so that the mysteries of the examination and its compounding difficulties may be eliminated or diminished by a sure method.

This book is meant to help you pass your examination provided that you qualify and are serious in your objective.

The entire field is reviewed through the huge store of content information which is succinctly presented through a provocative and challenging approach – the question-and-answer method.

A climate of success is established by furnishing the correct answers at the end of each test.

You soon learn to recognize types of questions, forms of questions, and patterns of questioning. You may even begin to anticipate expected outcomes.

You perceive that many questions are repeated or adapted so that you can gain acute insights, which may enable you to score many sure points.

You learn how to confront new questions, or types of questions, and to attack them confidently and work out the correct answers.

You note objectives and emphases, and recognize pitfalls and dangers, so that you may make positive educational adjustments.

Moreover, you are kept fully informed in relation to new concepts, methods, practices, and directions in the field.

You discover that you arre actually taking the examination all the time: you are preparing for the examination by "taking" an examination, not by reading extraneous and/or supererogatory textbooks.

In short, this PASSBOOK®, used directedly, should be an important factor in helping you to pass your test.

SENIOR CLERK-STENOGRAPHER

DUTIES
Performs difficult and responsible clerical, typing, and stenographic duties; performs related work as required.

SCOPE OF THE EXAMINATION
The written test will be designed to test for:
1. Vocabulary;
2. Proofreading;
3. Reading comprehension;
4. Arithmetic reasoning;
5. Record keeping;
6. Office equipment;
7. Secretarial practices; and
8. Supervision and training.

HOW TO TAKE A TEST

I. YOU MUST PASS AN EXAMINATION

A. WHAT EVERY CANDIDATE SHOULD KNOW

Examination applicants often ask us for help in preparing for the written test. What can I study in advance? What kinds of questions will be asked? How will the test be given? How will the papers be graded?

As an applicant for a civil service examination, you may be wondering about some of these things. Our purpose here is to suggest effective methods of advance study and to describe civil service examinations.

Your chances for success on this examination can be increased if you know how to prepare. Those "pre-examination jitters" can be reduced if you know what to expect. You can even experience an adventure in good citizenship if you know why civil service exams are given.

B. WHY ARE CIVIL SERVICE EXAMINATIONS GIVEN?

Civil service examinations are important to you in two ways. As a citizen, you want public jobs filled by employees who know how to do their work. As a job seeker, you want a fair chance to compete for that job on an equal footing with other candidates. The best-known means of accomplishing this two-fold goal is the competitive examination.

Exams are widely publicized throughout the nation. They may be administered for jobs in federal, state, city, municipal, town or village governments or agencies.

Any citizen may apply, with some limitations, such as the age or residence of applicants. Your experience and education may be reviewed to see whether you meet the requirements for the particular examination. When these requirements exist, they are reasonable and applied consistently to all applicants. Thus, a competitive examination may cause you some uneasiness now, but it is your privilege and safeguard.

C. HOW ARE CIVIL SERVICE EXAMS DEVELOPED?

Examinations are carefully written by trained technicians who are specialists in the field known as "psychological measurement," in consultation with recognized authorities in the field of work that the test will cover. These experts recommend the subject matter areas or skills to be tested; only those knowledges or skills important to your success on the job are included. The most reliable books and source materials available are used as references. Together, the experts and technicians judge the difficulty level of the questions.

Test technicians know how to phrase questions so that the problem is clearly stated. Their ethics do not permit "trick" or "catch" questions. Questions may have been tried out on sample groups, or subjected to statistical analysis, to determine their usefulness.

Written tests are often used in combination with performance tests, ratings of training and experience, and oral interviews. All of these measures combine to form the best-known means of finding the right person for the right job.

II. HOW TO PASS THE WRITTEN TEST

A. NATURE OF THE EXAMINATION

To prepare intelligently for civil service examinations, you should know how they differ from school examinations you have taken. In school you were assigned certain definite pages to read or subjects to cover. The examination questions were quite detailed and usually emphasized memory. Civil service exams, on the other hand, try to discover your present ability to perform the duties of a position, plus your potentiality to learn these duties. In other words, a civil service exam attempts to predict how successful you will be. Questions cover such a broad area that they cannot be as minute and detailed as school exam questions.

In the public service similar kinds of work, or positions, are grouped together in one "class." This process is known as *position-classification*. All the positions in a class are paid according to the salary range for that class. One class title covers all of these positions, and they are all tested by the same examination.

B. FOUR BASIC STEPS

1) Study the announcement

How, then, can you know what subjects to study? Our best answer is: "Learn as much as possible about the class of positions for which you've applied." The exam will test the knowledge, skills and abilities needed to do the work.

Your most valuable source of information about the position you want is the official exam announcement. This announcement lists the training and experience qualifications. Check these standards and apply only if you come reasonably close to meeting them.

The brief description of the position in the examination announcement offers some clues to the subjects which will be tested. Think about the job itself. Review the duties in your mind. Can you perform them, or are there some in which you are rusty? Fill in the blank spots in your preparation.

Many jurisdictions preview the written test in the exam announcement by including a section called "Knowledge and Abilities Required," "Scope of the Examination," or some similar heading. Here you will find out specifically what fields will be tested.

2) Review your own background

Once you learn in general what the position is all about, and what you need to know to do the work, ask yourself which subjects you already know fairly well and which need improvement. You may wonder whether to concentrate on improving your strong areas or on building some background in your fields of weakness. When the announcement has specified "some knowledge" or "considerable knowledge," or has used adjectives like "beginning principles of…" or "advanced … methods," you can get a clue as to the number and difficulty of questions to be asked in any given field. More questions, and hence broader coverage, would be included for those subjects which are more important in the work. Now weigh your strengths and weaknesses against the job requirements and prepare accordingly.

3) Determine the level of the position

Another way to tell how intensively you should prepare is to understand the level of the job for which you are applying. Is it the entering level? In other words, is this the position in which beginners in a field of work are hired? Or is it an intermediate or advanced level? Sometimes this is indicated by such words as "Junior" or "Senior" in the class title. Other jurisdictions use Roman numerals to designate the level – Clerk I, Clerk II, for example. The word "Supervisor" sometimes appears in the title. If the level is not indicated by the title, check the description of duties. Will you be working under very close supervision, or will you have responsibility for independent decisions in this work?

4) Choose appropriate study materials

Now that you know the subjects to be examined and the relative amount of each subject to be covered, you can choose suitable study materials. For beginning level jobs, or even advanced ones, if you have a pronounced weakness in some aspect of your training, read a modern, standard textbook in that field. Be sure it is up to date and has general coverage. Such books are normally available at your library, and the librarian will be glad to help you locate one. For entry-level positions, questions of appropriate difficulty are chosen – neither highly advanced questions, nor those too simple. Such questions require careful thought but not advanced training.

If the position for which you are applying is technical or advanced, you will read more advanced, specialized material. If you are already familiar with the basic principles of your field, elementary textbooks would waste your time. Concentrate on advanced textbooks and technical periodicals. Think through the concepts and review difficult problems in your field.

These are all general sources. You can get more ideas on your own initiative, following these leads. For example, training manuals and publications of the government agency which employs workers in your field can be useful, particularly for technical and professional positions. A letter or visit to the government department involved may result in more specific study suggestions, and certainly will provide you with a more definite idea of the exact nature of the position you are seeking.

III. KINDS OF TESTS

Tests are used for purposes other than measuring knowledge and ability to perform specified duties. For some positions, it is equally important to test ability to make adjustments to new situations or to profit from training. In others, basic mental abilities not dependent on information are essential. Questions which test these things may not appear as pertinent to the duties of the position as those which test for knowledge and information. Yet they are often highly important parts of a fair examination. For very general questions, it is almost impossible to help you direct your study efforts. What we can do is to point out some of the more common of these general abilities needed in public service positions and describe some typical questions.

1) General information

Broad, general information has been found useful for predicting job success in some kinds of work. This is tested in a variety of ways, from vocabulary lists to questions about current events. Basic background in some field of work, such as sociology or economics, may be sampled in a group of questions. Often these are principles which have become familiar to most persons through exposure rather than through formal training. It is difficult to advise you how to study for these questions; being alert to the world around you is our best suggestion.

2) Verbal ability

An example of an ability needed in many positions is verbal or language ability. Verbal ability is, in brief, the ability to use and understand words. Vocabulary and grammar tests are typical measures of this ability. Reading comprehension or paragraph interpretation questions are common in many kinds of civil service tests. You are given a paragraph of written material and asked to find its central meaning.

3) Numerical ability

Number skills can be tested by the familiar arithmetic problem, by checking paired lists of numbers to see which are alike and which are different, or by interpreting charts and graphs. In the latter test, a graph may be printed in the test booklet which you are asked to use as the basis for answering questions.

4) Observation

A popular test for law-enforcement positions is the observation test. A picture is shown to you for several minutes, then taken away. Questions about the picture test your ability to observe both details and larger elements.

5) Following directions

In many positions in the public service, the employee must be able to carry out written instructions dependably and accurately. You may be given a chart with several columns, each column listing a variety of information. The questions require you to carry out directions involving the information given in the chart.

6) Skills and aptitudes

Performance tests effectively measure some manual skills and aptitudes. When the skill is one in which you are trained, such as typing or shorthand, you can practice. These tests are often very much like those given in business school or high school courses. For many of the other skills and aptitudes, however, no short-time preparation can be made. Skills and abilities natural to you or that you have developed throughout your lifetime are being tested.

Many of the general questions just described provide all the data needed to answer the questions and ask you to use your reasoning ability to find the answers. Your best preparation for these tests, as well as for tests of facts and ideas, is to be at your physical and mental best. You, no doubt, have your own methods of getting into an exam-taking mood and keeping "in shape." The next section lists some ideas on this subject.

IV. KINDS OF QUESTIONS

Only rarely is the "essay" question, which you answer in narrative form, used in civil service tests. Civil service tests are usually of the short-answer type. Full instructions for answering these questions will be given to you at the examination. But in case this is your first experience with short-answer questions and separate answer sheets, here is what you need to know:

1) Multiple-choice Questions

Most popular of the short-answer questions is the "multiple choice" or "best answer" question. It can be used, for example, to test for factual knowledge, ability to solve problems or judgment in meeting situations found at work.

A multiple-choice question is normally one of three types—

- It can begin with an incomplete statement followed by several possible endings. You are to find the one ending which *best* completes the statement, although some of the others may not be entirely wrong.
- It can also be a complete statement in the form of a question which is answered by choosing one of the statements listed.
- It can be in the form of a problem – again you select the best answer.

Here is an example of a multiple-choice question with a discussion which should give you some clues as to the method for choosing the right answer:

When an employee has a complaint about his assignment, the action which will *best* help him overcome his difficulty is to
  A. discuss his difficulty with his coworkers
  B. take the problem to the head of the organization
  C. take the problem to the person who gave him the assignment
  D. say nothing to anyone about his complaint

In answering this question, you should study each of the choices to find which is best. Consider choice "A" – Certainly an employee may discuss his complaint with fellow employees, but no change or improvement can result, and the complaint remains unresolved. Choice "B" is a poor choice since the head of the organization probably does not know what assignment you have been given, and taking your problem to him is known as "going over the head" of the supervisor. The supervisor, or person who made the assignment, is the person who can clarify it or correct any injustice. Choice "C" is, therefore, correct. To say nothing, as in choice "D," is unwise. Supervisors have and interest in knowing the problems employees are facing, and the employee is seeking a solution to his problem.

2) True/False Questions

The "true/false" or "right/wrong" form of question is sometimes used. Here a complete statement is given. Your job is to decide whether the statement is right or wrong.

SAMPLE: A roaming cell-phone call to a nearby city costs less than a non-roaming call to a distant city.

This statement is wrong, or false, since roaming calls are more expensive.
This is not a complete list of all possible question forms, although most of the others are variations of these common types. You will always get complete directions for

answering questions. Be sure you understand *how* to mark your answers – ask questions until you do.

V. RECORDING YOUR ANSWERS

Computer terminals are used more and more today for many different kinds of exams.

For an examination with very few applicants, you may be told to record your answers in the test booklet itself. Separate answer sheets are much more common. If this separate answer sheet is to be scored by machine – and this is often the case – it is highly important that you mark your answers correctly in order to get credit.

An electronic scoring machine is often used in civil service offices because of the speed with which papers can be scored. Machine-scored answer sheets must be marked with a pencil, which will be given to you. This pencil has a high graphite content which responds to the electronic scoring machine. As a matter of fact, stray dots may register as answers, so do not let your pencil rest on the answer sheet while you are pondering the correct answer. Also, if your pencil lead breaks or is otherwise defective, ask for another.

Since the answer sheet will be dropped in a slot in the scoring machine, be careful not to bend the corners or get the paper crumpled.

The answer sheet normally has five vertical columns of numbers, with 30 numbers to a column. These numbers correspond to the question numbers in your test booklet. After each number, going across the page are four or five pairs of dotted lines. These short dotted lines have small letters or numbers above them. The first two pairs may also have a "T" or "F" above the letters. This indicates that the first two pairs only are to be used if the questions are of the true-false type. If the questions are multiple choice, disregard the "T" and "F" and pay attention only to the small letters or numbers.

Answer your questions in the manner of the sample that follows:

32. The largest city in the United States is
    A. Washington, D.C.
    B. New York City
    C. Chicago
    D. Detroit
    E. San Francisco

1) Choose the answer you think is best. (New York City is the largest, so "B" is correct.)
2) Find the row of dotted lines numbered the same as the question you are answering. (Find row number 32)
3) Find the pair of dotted lines corresponding to the answer. (Find the pair of lines under the mark "B.")
4) Make a solid black mark between the dotted lines.

VI. BEFORE THE TEST

Common sense will help you find procedures to follow to get ready for an examination. Too many of us, however, overlook these sensible measures. Indeed, nervousness and fatigue have been found to be the most serious reasons why applicants fail to do their best on civil service tests. Here is a list of reminders:

- Begin your preparation early – Don't wait until the last minute to go scurrying around for books and materials or to find out what the position is all about.
- Prepare continuously – An hour a night for a week is better than an all-night cram session. This has been definitely established. What is more, a night a week for a month will return better dividends than crowding your study into a shorter period of time.
- Locate the place of the exam – You have been sent a notice telling you when and where to report for the examination. If the location is in a different town or otherwise unfamiliar to you, it would be well to inquire the best route and learn something about the building.
- Relax the night before the test – Allow your mind to rest. Do not study at all that night. Plan some mild recreation or diversion; then go to bed early and get a good night's sleep.
- Get up early enough to make a leisurely trip to the place for the test – This way unforeseen events, traffic snarls, unfamiliar buildings, etc. will not upset you.
- Dress comfortably – A written test is not a fashion show. You will be known by number and not by name, so wear something comfortable.
- Leave excess paraphernalia at home – Shopping bags and odd bundles will get in your way. You need bring only the items mentioned in the official notice you received; usually everything you need is provided. Do not bring reference books to the exam. They will only confuse those last minutes and be taken away from you when in the test room.
- Arrive somewhat ahead of time – If because of transportation schedules you must get there very early, bring a newspaper or magazine to take your mind off yourself while waiting.
- Locate the examination room – When you have found the proper room, you will be directed to the seat or part of the room where you will sit. Sometimes you are given a sheet of instructions to read while you are waiting. Do not fill out any forms until you are told to do so; just read them and be prepared.
- Relax and prepare to listen to the instructions
- If you have any physical problem that may keep you from doing your best, be sure to tell the test administrator. If you are sick or in poor health, you really cannot do your best on the exam. You can come back and take the test some other time.

VII. AT THE TEST

The day of the test is here and you have the test booklet in your hand. The temptation to get going is very strong. Caution! There is more to success than knowing the right answers. You must know how to identify your papers and understand variations in the type of short-answer question used in this particular examination. Follow these suggestions for maximum results from your efforts:

1) Cooperate with the monitor

The test administrator has a duty to create a situation in which you can be as much at ease as possible. He will give instructions, tell you when to begin, check to see that you are marking your answer sheet correctly, and so on. He is not there to guard you, although he will see that your competitors do not take unfair advantage. He wants to help you do your best.

2) Listen to all instructions

Don't jump the gun! Wait until you understand all directions. In most civil service tests you get more time than you need to answer the questions. So don't be in a hurry. Read each word of instructions until you clearly understand the meaning. Study the examples, listen to all announcements and follow directions. Ask questions if you do not understand what to do.

3) Identify your papers

Civil service exams are usually identified by number only. You will be assigned a number; you must not put your name on your test papers. Be sure to copy your number correctly. Since more than one exam may be given, copy your exact examination title.

4) Plan your time

Unless you are told that a test is a "speed" or "rate of work" test, speed itself is usually not important. Time enough to answer all the questions will be provided, but this does not mean that you have all day. An overall time limit has been set. Divide the total time (in minutes) by the number of questions to determine the approximate time you have for each question.

5) Do not linger over difficult questions

If you come across a difficult question, mark it with a paper clip (useful to have along) and come back to it when you have been through the booklet. One caution if you do this – be sure to skip a number on your answer sheet as well. Check often to be sure that you have not lost your place and that you are marking in the row numbered the same as the question you are answering.

6) Read the questions

Be sure you know what the question asks! Many capable people are unsuccessful because they failed to *read* the questions correctly.

7) Answer all questions

Unless you have been instructed that a penalty will be deducted for incorrect answers, it is better to guess than to omit a question.

8) Speed tests

It is often better NOT to guess on speed tests. It has been found that on timed tests people are tempted to spend the last few seconds before time is called in marking answers at random – without even reading them – in the hope of picking up a few extra points. To discourage this practice, the instructions may warn you that your score will be "corrected" for guessing. That is, a penalty will be applied. The incorrect answers will be deducted from the correct ones, or some other penalty formula will be used.

9) Review your answers

If you finish before time is called, go back to the questions you guessed or omitted to give them further thought. Review other answers if you have time.

10) Return your test materials

If you are ready to leave before others have finished or time is called, take ALL your materials to the monitor and leave quietly. Never take any test material with you. The monitor can discover whose papers are not complete, and taking a test booklet may be grounds for disqualification.

VIII. EXAMINATION TECHNIQUES

1) Read the general instructions carefully. These are usually printed on the first page of the exam booklet. As a rule, these instructions refer to the timing of the examination; the fact that you should not start work until the signal and must stop work at a signal, etc. If there are any *special* instructions, such as a choice of questions to be answered, make sure that you note this instruction carefully.

2) When you are ready to start work on the examination, that is as soon as the signal has been given, read the instructions to each question booklet, underline any key words or phrases, such as *least, best, outline, describe* and the like. In this way you will tend to answer as requested rather than discover on reviewing your paper that you *listed without describing*, that you selected the *worst* choice rather than the *best* choice, etc.

3) If the examination is of the objective or multiple-choice type – that is, each question will also give a series of possible answers: A, B, C or D, and you are called upon to select the best answer and write the letter next to that answer on your answer paper – it is advisable to start answering each question in turn. There may be anywhere from 50 to 100 such questions in the three or four hours allotted and you can see how much time would be taken if you read through all the questions before beginning to answer any. Furthermore, if you come across a question or group of questions which you know would be difficult to answer, it would undoubtedly affect your handling of all the other questions.

4) If the examination is of the essay type and contains but a few questions, it is a moot point as to whether you should read all the questions before starting to answer any one. Of course, if you are given a choice – say five out of seven and the like – then it is essential to read all the questions so you can eliminate the two that are most difficult. If, however, you are asked to answer all the questions, there may be danger in trying to answer the easiest one first because you may find that you will spend too much time on it. The best technique is to answer the first question, then proceed to the second, etc.

5) Time your answers. Before the exam begins, write down the time it started, then add the time allowed for the examination and write down the time it must be completed, then divide the time available somewhat as follows:

- If 3-1/2 hours are allowed, that would be 210 minutes. If you have 80 objective-type questions, that would be an average of 2-1/2 minutes per question. Allow yourself no more than 2 minutes per question, or a total of 160 minutes, which will permit about 50 minutes to review.
- If for the time allotment of 210 minutes there are 7 essay questions to answer, that would average about 30 minutes a question. Give yourself only 25 minutes per question so that you have about 35 minutes to review.

6) The most important instruction is to *read each question* and make sure you know what is wanted. The second most important instruction is to *time yourself properly* so that you answer every question. The third most important instruction is to *answer every question*. Guess if you have to but include something for each question. Remember that you will receive no credit for a blank and will probably receive some credit if you write something in answer to an essay question. If you guess a letter – say "B" for a multiple-choice question – you may have guessed right. If you leave a blank as an answer to a multiple-choice question, the examiners may respect your feelings but it will not add a point to your score. Some exams may penalize you for wrong answers, so in such cases *only*, you may not want to guess unless you have some basis for your answer.

7) Suggestions
   a. Objective-type questions
      1. Examine the question booklet for proper sequence of pages and questions
      2. Read all instructions carefully
      3. Skip any question which seems too difficult; return to it after all other questions have been answered
      4. Apportion your time properly; do not spend too much time on any single question or group of questions
      5. Note and underline key words – *all, most, fewest, least, best, worst, same, opposite,* etc.
      6. Pay particular attention to negatives
      7. Note unusual option, e.g., unduly long, short, complex, different or similar in content to the body of the question
      8. Observe the use of "hedging" words – *probably, may, most likely,* etc.
      9. Make sure that your answer is put next to the same number as the question
      10. Do not second-guess unless you have good reason to believe the second answer is definitely more correct
      11. Cross out original answer if you decide another answer is more accurate; do not erase until you are ready to hand your paper in
      12. Answer all questions; guess unless instructed otherwise
      13. Leave time for review

   b. Essay questions
      1. Read each question carefully
      2. Determine exactly what is wanted. Underline key words or phrases.
      3. Decide on outline or paragraph answer

4. Include many different points and elements unless asked to develop any one or two points or elements
5. Show impartiality by giving pros and cons unless directed to select one side only
6. Make and write down any assumptions you find necessary to answer the questions
7. Watch your English, grammar, punctuation and choice of words
8. Time your answers; don't crowd material

8) Answering the essay question

Most essay questions can be answered by framing the specific response around several key words or ideas. Here are a few such key words or ideas:

M's: manpower, materials, methods, money, management
P's: purpose, program, policy, plan, procedure, practice, problems, pitfalls, personnel, public relations

  a. Six basic steps in handling problems:
    1. Preliminary plan and background development
    2. Collect information, data and facts
    3. Analyze and interpret information, data and facts
    4. Analyze and develop solutions as well as make recommendations
    5. Prepare report and sell recommendations
    6. Install recommendations and follow up effectiveness

  b. Pitfalls to avoid
    1. *Taking things for granted* – A statement of the situation does not necessarily imply that each of the elements is necessarily true; for example, a complaint may be invalid and biased so that all that can be taken for granted is that a complaint has been registered
    2. *Considering only one side of a situation* – Wherever possible, indicate several alternatives and then point out the reasons you selected the best one
    3. *Failing to indicate follow up* – Whenever your answer indicates action on your part, make certain that you will take proper follow-up action to see how successful your recommendations, procedures or actions turn out to be
    4. *Taking too long in answering any single question* – Remember to time your answers properly

IX. AFTER THE TEST

Scoring procedures differ in detail among civil service jurisdictions although the general principles are the same. Whether the papers are hand-scored or graded by machine we have described, they are nearly always graded by number. That is, the person who marks the paper knows only the number – never the name – of the applicant. Not until all the papers have been graded will they be matched with names. If other tests, such as training and experience or oral interview ratings have been given, scores will be combined. Different parts of the examination usually have different weights. For example, the written test might count 60 percent of the final grade, and a rating of training and experience 40 percent. In many jurisdictions, veterans will have a certain number of points added to their grades.

After the final grade has been determined, the names are placed in grade order and an eligible list is established. There are various methods for resolving ties between those who get the same final grade – probably the most common is to place first the name of the person whose application was received first. Job offers are made from the eligible list in the order the names appear on it. You will be notified of your grade and your rank as soon as all these computations have been made. This will be done as rapidly as possible.

People who are found to meet the requirements in the announcement are called "eligibles." Their names are put on a list of eligible candidates. An eligible's chances of getting a job depend on how high he stands on this list and how fast agencies are filling jobs from the list.

When a job is to be filled from a list of eligibles, the agency asks for the names of people on the list of eligibles for that job. When the civil service commission receives this request, it sends to the agency the names of the three people highest on this list. Or, if the job to be filled has specialized requirements, the office sends the agency the names of the top three persons who meet these requirements from the general list.

The appointing officer makes a choice from among the three people whose names were sent to him. If the selected person accepts the appointment, the names of the others are put back on the list to be considered for future openings.

That is the rule in hiring from all kinds of eligible lists, whether they are for typist, carpenter, chemist, or something else. For every vacancy, the appointing officer has his choice of any one of the top three eligibles on the list. This explains why the person whose name is on top of the list sometimes does not get an appointment when some of the persons lower on the list do. If the appointing officer chooses the second or third eligible, the No. 1 eligible does not get a job at once, but stays on the list until he is appointed or the list is terminated.

X. HOW TO PASS THE INTERVIEW TEST

The examination for which you applied requires an oral interview test. You have already taken the written test and you are now being called for the interview test – the final part of the formal examination.

You may think that it is not possible to prepare for an interview test and that there are no procedures to follow during an interview. Our purpose is to point out some things you can do in advance that will help you and some good rules to follow and pitfalls to avoid while you are being interviewed.

What is an interview supposed to test?

The written examination is designed to test the technical knowledge and competence of the candidate; the oral is designed to evaluate intangible qualities, not readily measured otherwise, and to establish a list showing the relative fitness of each candidate – as measured against his competitors – for the position sought. Scoring is not on the basis of "right" and "wrong," but on a sliding scale of values ranging from "not passable" to "outstanding." As a matter of fact, it is possible to achieve a relatively low score without a single "incorrect" answer because of evident weakness in the qualities being measured.

Occasionally, an examination may consist entirely of an oral test – either an individual or a group oral. In such cases, information is sought concerning the technical knowledges and abilities of the candidate, since there has been no written examination for this purpose. More commonly, however, an oral test is used to supplement a written examination.

Who conducts interviews?

The composition of oral boards varies among different jurisdictions. In nearly all, a representative of the personnel department serves as chairman. One of the members of the board may be a representative of the department in which the candidate would work. In some cases, "outside experts" are used, and, frequently, a businessman or some other representative of the general public is asked to serve. Labor and management or other special groups may be represented. The aim is to secure the services of experts in the appropriate field.

However the board is composed, it is a good idea (and not at all improper or unethical) to ascertain in advance of the interview who the members are and what groups they represent. When you are introduced to them, you will have some idea of their backgrounds and interests, and at least you will not stutter and stammer over their names.

What should be done before the interview?

While knowledge about the board members is useful and takes some of the surprise element out of the interview, there is other preparation which is more substantive. It *is* possible to prepare for an oral interview – in several ways:

1) Keep a copy of your application and review it carefully before the interview

This may be the only document before the oral board, and the starting point of the interview. Know what education and experience you have listed there, and the sequence and dates of all of it. Sometimes the board will ask you to review the highlights of your experience for them; you should not have to hem and haw doing it.

2) Study the class specification and the examination announcement

Usually, the oral board has one or both of these to guide them. The qualities, characteristics or knowledges required by the position sought are stated in these documents. They offer valuable clues as to the nature of the oral interview. For example, if the job involves supervisory responsibilities, the announcement will usually indicate that knowledge of modern supervisory methods and the qualifications of the candidate as a supervisor will be tested. If so, you can expect such questions, frequently in the form of a hypothetical situation which you are expected to solve. NEVER go into an oral without knowledge of the duties and responsibilities of the job you seek.

3) Think through each qualification required

Try to visualize the kind of questions you would ask if you were a board member. How well could you answer them? Try especially to appraise your own knowledge and background in each area, *measured against the job sought*, and identify any areas in which you are weak. Be critical and realistic – do not flatter yourself.

4) Do some general reading in areas in which you feel you may be weak

For example, if the job involves supervision and your past experience has NOT, some general reading in supervisory methods and practices, particularly in the field of human relations, might be useful. Do NOT study agency procedures or detailed manuals. The oral board will be testing your understanding and capacity, not your memory.

5) Get a good night's sleep and watch your general health and mental attitude

You will want a clear head at the interview. Take care of a cold or any other minor ailment, and of course, no hangovers.

What should be done on the day of the interview?

Now comes the day of the interview itself. Give yourself plenty of time to get there. Plan to arrive somewhat ahead of the scheduled time, particularly if your appointment is in the fore part of the day. If a previous candidate fails to appear, the board might be ready for you a bit early. By early afternoon an oral board is almost invariably behind schedule if there are many candidates, and you may have to wait. Take along a book or magazine to read, or your application to review, but leave any extraneous material in the waiting room when you go in for your interview. In any event, relax and compose yourself.

The matter of dress is important. The board is forming impressions about you – from your experience, your manners, your attitude, and your appearance. Give your personal appearance careful attention. Dress your best, but not your flashiest. Choose conservative, appropriate clothing, and be sure it is immaculate. This is a business interview, and your appearance should indicate that you regard it as such. Besides, being well groomed and properly dressed will help boost your confidence.

Sooner or later, someone will call your name and escort you into the interview room. *This is it.* From here on you are on your own. It is too late for any more preparation. But remember, you asked for this opportunity to prove your fitness, and you are here because your request was granted.

What happens when you go in?

The usual sequence of events will be as follows: The clerk (who is often the board stenographer) will introduce you to the chairman of the oral board, who will introduce you to the other members of the board. Acknowledge the introductions before you sit down. Do not be surprised if you find a microphone facing you or a stenotypist sitting by. Oral interviews are usually recorded in the event of an appeal or other review.

Usually the chairman of the board will open the interview by reviewing the highlights of your education and work experience from your application – primarily for the benefit of the other members of the board, as well as to get the material into the record. Do not interrupt or comment unless there is an error or significant misinterpretation; if that is the case, do not hesitate. But do not quibble about insignificant matters. Also, he will usually ask you some question about your education, experience or your present job – partly to get you to start talking and to establish the interviewing "rapport." He may start the actual questioning, or turn it over to one of the other members. Frequently, each member undertakes the questioning on a particular area, one in which he is perhaps most competent, so you can expect each member to participate in the examination. Because time is limited, you may also expect some rather abrupt switches in the direction the questioning takes, so do not be upset by it. Normally, a board member will not pursue a single line of questioning unless he discovers a particular strength or weakness.

After each member has participated, the chairman will usually ask whether any member has any further questions, then will ask you if you have anything you wish to add. Unless you are expecting this question, it may floor you. Worse, it may start you off on an extended, extemporaneous speech. The board is not usually seeking more information. The question is principally to offer you a last opportunity to present further qualifications or to indicate that you have nothing to add. So, if you feel that a significant qualification or characteristic has been overlooked, it is proper to point it out in a sentence or so. Do not compliment the board on the thoroughness of their examination – they have been sketchy, and you know it. If you wish, merely say, "No thank you, I have nothing further to add." This is a point where you can "talk yourself out" of a good impression or fail to present an important bit of information. Remember, *you close the interview yourself.*

The chairman will then say, "That is all, Mr. _____, thank you." Do not be startled; the interview is over, and quicker than you think. Thank him, gather your belongings and take your leave. Save your sigh of relief for the other side of the door.

How to put your best foot forward

Throughout this entire process, you may feel that the board individually and collectively is trying to pierce your defenses, seek out your hidden weaknesses and embarrass and confuse you. Actually, this is not true. They are obliged to make an appraisal of your qualifications for the job you are seeking, and they want to see you in your best light. Remember, they must interview all candidates and a non-cooperative candidate may become a failure in spite of their best efforts to bring out his qualifications. Here are 15 suggestions that will help you:

1) Be natural – Keep your attitude confident, not cocky

If you are not confident that you can do the job, do not expect the board to be. Do not apologize for your weaknesses, try to bring out your strong points. The board is interested in a positive, not negative, presentation. Cockiness will antagonize any board member and make him wonder if you are covering up a weakness by a false show of strength.

2) Get comfortable, but don't lounge or sprawl

Sit erectly but not stiffly. A careless posture may lead the board to conclude that you are careless in other things, or at least that you are not impressed by the importance of the occasion. Either conclusion is natural, even if incorrect. Do not fuss with your clothing, a pencil or an ashtray. Your hands may occasionally be useful to emphasize a point; do not let them become a point of distraction.

3) Do not wisecrack or make small talk

This is a serious situation, and your attitude should show that you consider it as such. Further, the time of the board is limited – they do not want to waste it, and neither should you.

4) Do not exaggerate your experience or abilities

In the first place, from information in the application or other interviews and sources, the board may know more about you than you think. Secondly, you probably will not get away with it. An experienced board is rather adept at spotting such a situation, so do not take the chance.

5) If you know a board member, do not make a point of it, yet do not hide it

Certainly you are not fooling him, and probably not the other members of the board. Do not try to take advantage of your acquaintanceship – it will probably do you little good.

6) Do not dominate the interview

Let the board do that. They will give you the clues – do not assume that you have to do all the talking. Realize that the board has a number of questions to ask you, and do not try to take up all the interview time by showing off your extensive knowledge of the answer to the first one.

7) Be attentive

You only have 20 minutes or so, and you should keep your attention at its sharpest throughout. When a member is addressing a problem or question to you, give him your undivided attention. Address your reply principally to him, but do not exclude the other board members.

8) Do not interrupt

A board member may be stating a problem for you to analyze. He will ask you a question when the time comes. Let him state the problem, and wait for the question.

9) Make sure you understand the question

Do not try to answer until you are sure what the question is. If it is not clear, restate it in your own words or ask the board member to clarify it for you. However, do not haggle about minor elements.

10) Reply promptly but not hastily

A common entry on oral board rating sheets is "candidate responded readily," or "candidate hesitated in replies." Respond as promptly and quickly as you can, but do not jump to a hasty, ill-considered answer.

11) Do not be peremptory in your answers

A brief answer is proper – but do not fire your answer back. That is a losing game from your point of view. The board member can probably ask questions much faster than you can answer them.

12) Do not try to create the answer you think the board member wants

He is interested in what kind of mind you have and how it works – not in playing games. Furthermore, he can usually spot this practice and will actually grade you down on it.

13) Do not switch sides in your reply merely to agree with a board member

Frequently, a member will take a contrary position merely to draw you out and to see if you are willing and able to defend your point of view. Do not start a debate, yet do not surrender a good position. If a position is worth taking, it is worth defending.

14) Do not be afraid to admit an error in judgment if you are shown to be wrong

The board knows that you are forced to reply without any opportunity for careful consideration. Your answer may be demonstrably wrong. If so, admit it and get on with the interview.

15) Do not dwell at length on your present job

The opening question may relate to your present assignment. Answer the question but do not go into an extended discussion. You are being examined for a *new* job, not your present one. As a matter of fact, try to phrase ALL your answers in terms of the job for which you are being examined.

Basis of Rating

Probably you will forget most of these "do's" and "don'ts" when you walk into the oral interview room. Even remembering them all will not ensure you a passing grade. Perhaps you did not have the qualifications in the first place. But remembering them will help you to put your best foot forward, without treading on the toes of the board members.

Rumor and popular opinion to the contrary notwithstanding, an oral board wants you to make the best appearance possible. They know you are under pressure – but they also want to see how you respond to it as a guide to what your reaction would be under the pressures of the job you seek. They will be influenced by the degree of poise you display, the personal traits you show and the manner in which you respond.

ABOUT THIS BOOK

This book contains tests divided into Examination Sections. Go through each test, answering every question in the margin. At the end of each test look at the answer key and check your answers. On the ones you got wrong, look at the right answer choice and learn. Do not fill in the answers first. Do not memorize the questions and answers, but understand the answer and principles involved. On your test, the questions will likely be different from the samples. Questions are changed and new ones added. If you understand these past questions you should have success with any changes that arise. Tests may consist of several types of questions. We have additional books on each subject should more study be advisable or necessary for you. Finally, the more you study, the better prepared you will be. This book is intended to be the last thing you study before you walk into the examination room. Prior study of relevant texts is also recommended. NLC publishes some of these in our Fundamental Series. Knowledge and good sense are important factors in passing your exam. Good luck also helps. So now study this Passbook, absorb the material contained within and take that knowledge into the examination. Then do your best to pass that exam.

EXAMINATION SECTION

HOW TO PREPARE FOR THE BASIC SKILL SUBJECTS
ARITHMETIC, VOCABULARY, GRAMMARY, SUPERVISION

Preparing for an examination is an individual process. It depends on the job description, examination announcement, and on your own knowledge and skills. A study of previous examinations and the examination announcement should give you an idea of the kinds of questions you may get; however, developing the various skills in arithmetic, grammar, vocabulary, and supervision needed to answer the questions can be done only by you.

We have listed below some examples relating to these skills which you may need to pass a clerical/supervisory examination. Work out the examples below; if you have difficulty with any one of them, you know that you should definitely go further into the subject. Even if you can do these examples easily, you should review previous examinations for other kinds of problems that may give you difficulty. In any case, you should determine the areas in which you are weak and concentrate your efforts on them. After doing these questions, see whether your answers and methods match the solutions and key answers at the end of this section.

I.   ARITHMETIC

1. An office is 12 feet long and 15 feet wide. What will be the cost of covering the floor wall to wall with carpet that sells for $9.00 a square yard.

2. A stenographer spends 13 hours typing, 4 hours taking dictation, and one-fifth of the time filing. What percentage of her time does she spend on miscellaneous duties if she works a 40-hour week?

3. A clerk, who can do $2\frac{1}{4}\%$ of a card-filing job in one hour, works at the rate of 630 cards per hour. How many card must he file to complete the job?

Were you able to do the above easily? In preparing for an examination which may include arithmetic problems, it is essential that you first review your basic arithmetical operations such as addition, subtraction, multiplication, and division of whole numbers, percentages, fractions, and decimals. A 6th- or 7th-year school text will probably give you all the review you need in these fundamentals. After you review the fundamentals, then apply your knowledge to the kind of questions normally given on the examination for which you are preparing.

II. VOCABULARY

fractious	conductive
functional	congruous
officious	contingent

Did you find these words difficult? If you did, you should do something about improving your vocabulary because these are words that came from previous examinations. Again, it is good to go back to fundamentals. Get into the habit of looking up any word you come across in your reading that you don't know, particularly words that have some relationship to the subject matter of your examination. In examinations for Police Officer, words like duress, indictment, contempt, and deter are used because they have to do, in one form or another, with police action. On the same basis, if you are preparing for a clerical-administrative examination, you should be familiar with the words listed above.

III. GRAMMAR

1. Entering the office, the desk was noticed immediately by the visitor.

2. The office manager estimates that the job, which is to be handled by you and I, will require about two weeks for completion.

3. The supervisor knew that the typist was a quiet, cooperative, efficient, employee.

4. We do not know who you have designated to take charge of the new program.

5. Neither Mr. Smith nor Mr. Jones were able to do their assignment on time.

Did you know what was incorrect in the above sentences? These examples came from previous examinations and reflect common errors in grammar and correct usage. If you had any difficulty with these examples, then a review of basic grammatical and punctuation rules is in order. Look through the grammar questions in the examinations included in this book; you will see that certain errors are repeated in each examination. Stress is placed on such principles as agreement between subject and verb, use of the objective form of the pronoun after a preposition, correct use of who or whom, and the punctuation needed for a restrictive or non-restrictive clause. Your studying, therefore, should be geared to a review of these principles.

IV. SUPERVISION

1. Of the following, the one which is NOT a good rule in disciplining subordinates is for a supervisor to
   A. be as specific as possible in criticizing a subordinate for his faults
   B. allow an extended period to elapse after an error has been committed before reprimanding the offending employee
   C. be sure he has all the facts before reprimanding an employee for an error he has committed
   D. reprimand the employee in private even though the fault was committed publicly

2. "Unity of command" requires that
   A. all units perform the same operation in the same manner
   B. managers comply with established policy at all times
   C. orders be issued through the established line of authority
   D. managers be in general agreement on policy

3. It is generally best that the greater part of in-service training for the operating employees of an agency in a pubic jurisdiction be given by
   A. a team of trainers from the central personnel agency of the jurisdiction
   B. training specialists on the staff of the personnel unit of the agency
   C. a team of teachers from the public school system of the jurisdiction
   D. members of the regular supervisory force of the agency

4. Studies of organizations show that formal employee participation in the formulation of work policies before they are put into effect is most likely to result in
   A. a reduction in the length of time required to formulate the policies
   B. an increase in the number of employees affected by the policies
   C. a reduction in the length of time required to implement the policies
   D. an increase in the number of policies formulated within the organization

Did you understand what supervisory principles were involved in the above examples? If not, then a review of supervision is in order. Examinations tend to stress the role of a supervisor as a leader who has understanding of human relations and leadership principles. If you feel a need for a refresher in this area, almost any one of the books on this area listed in our catalog should be of help to you.

———————

SOLUTIONS/EXPLANATIONS OF ANSWERS

I. ARITHMETIC

1. This problem requires you to know the basic formula for measuring the area of a rectangle (Area = Length x Width) and involves the elementary arithmetical processes of multiplication and division.

   First, change the dimensions from feet to yards because the statement indicates that the cost is to be expressed in yards. Since there are 3 feet in a yard, divide the number of feet by 3 to get yards.

   $$\frac{12 \text{ ft. wide}}{3 \text{ ft. in a yard}} = 4 \text{ yards} \qquad \frac{15 \text{ ft. long}}{3 \text{ ft. in a yard}} = 5 \text{ yards}$$

   4 yards x 5 yards =   20 sq. yards needed

                           x$9.00 cost per square yard

                    $180.00 cost to cover floor wall to wall

2. This problem requires you to know how to use fractions and how to convert fractions to percentages.

   First, find in hours the equivalent of "1/5 of the time filing."

   (Multiplying by a fraction) 1/5 x 40 hrs. = time filing = 8

                               1/5 x 40 hrs. = 8 hrs. filing

                                            13 hrs. typing

                                            _4 hrs. dictation

                                          25 hrs. for above duties

                           40 hrs. work

                        -25 hrs. accounted for, as above

                        15 hrs. for miscellaneous duties

   $$\frac{15}{40} = 3/8$$

   (To get % multiply the fraction x 100) $3/8 \times 100 = \dfrac{300}{8} = 37\frac{1}{2}\%$

3. Rephrase the statement in your mind to read 2¼% of the total equals 6t30 cards. If 630 cards are done in 1 hour, and that represents 2¼% of the total number of cards, then

                   2¼% of total = 630

                         or

                   $\frac{9}{4}\%$ of total = 630

(Change percent to
fraction by dividing
by 100)

$$\frac{9}{400} \text{ of total} = 630$$

$$\text{Total} = 630 \times \frac{400}{9}$$

$$\text{Total} = \frac{252000}{9}$$

$$\text{Total} = 28000 \text{ cards}$$

II. VOCABULARY

The improvement of vocabulary requires intensive and extensive study of words and their meanings.

It is impossible to treat this area adequately in this brief overview.

The best preparation is to secure the book on vocabulary, listed under the heading Basic/General Education, in this catalog.

III. GRAMMAR

1. This sentence is incorrect because we don't know who entered the office. The sentence, as it stands, has a dangling participle, "entering." It indicates that the desk entered the office, which, obviously, is not so. It would be correct to say "Entering the office, the visitor noticed the desk immediately." Then, there is no question about who entered the office.

2. As you probably noted, the sentence should have read "you and me" following the preposition by instead of "you and I." Prepositions such as by, between, etc. are followed by the objective form of the pronoun—me, him, her, us, and them.

3. This sentence has a punctuation error. No comma is ever placed between the adjective and the noun it modifies. The comma after "efficient" is incorrect. The sentence should read: "The supervisor knew that the typist was a quiet, cooperative, and efficient employee."

4. The sentence should have "whom" instead of "who." What is needed is an object to the verb "designated" and, therefore, "whom," the objective form of the pronoun, is used.

5. The sentence is incorrect because the verb "were" should apply to Mr. Jones, the nearer subject. Following a correlative conjunction such as neither-nor or either-or, the verb should be singular.

IV. SUPERVISION

1. <u>Answer B</u>: Always remember that in answering a question of this type, three of the four choices will probably be GOOD rules to follow in discipline.

   Answers A, C, and D ARE good so that leaves B.

   B is NOT good rule for several reasons:
   1. If you allow an extended period to elapse, both you and he may have FORGOTTEN the incident.
   2. He'll probably be making more of the same errors.
   3. Discipline, as a corrective device, is most helpful when the incident or error is fresh in the employee's mind.
   4. The employee may wonder why you waited. He may think you are using this instance as a means of "picking on" him for something else he did or for personal dislike.

2. <u>Answer C</u>: Unity of command by DEFINITION means the organizational setup whereby authority and orders follow definite chains or lines of authority. (Look at a typical organization chart.) An important concept associated with this principle is that no member of an organization reports to more than one supervisor.

3. <u>Answer D</u>: Note the wording of the question—"greater part." This question tests your recognition of the principle that one of the supervisor's basic functions is that of employee training and that the regular supervisor in the agency is in the best position to determine what the employee needs to know in order to perform the type, quality, and quantity of work required.

4. <u>Answer C</u>: This answer brings out one of the important forces at work in human relations. People like to participate in preparing plans that may affect them and will, therefore, cooperate more fully in implementing the plans.

EXAMINATION SECTION
TEST 1

DIRECTIONS: Each question or incomplete statement is followed by several suggested answers or completions. Select the one that BEST answers the question or completes the statement. *PRINT THE LETTER OF THE CORRECT ANSWER IN THE SPACE AT THE RIGHT.*

1. When you select someone to serve as supervisor of your unit during your absence on vacation and at other times, it would generally be BEST to choose the employee who is

    A. able to move the work along smoothly without friction
    B. on staff longest
    C. liked best by the rest of the staff
    D. able to perform the work of each employee to be supervised

2. Successful supervision of handicapped persons employed in a department depends MOST on providing them with a work place and work climate

    A. which is safe and accident-free
    B. that requires close and direct supervision by others
    C. that requires the performance of routine, repetitive tasks under a minimum of pressure
    D. where they will be accepted by the other employees

3. Studies have indicated that when employees feel that their work is aimless and unchallenging, the allocation or payment of more money for this type of work is LIKELY to

    A. contribute little to increased production
    B. bring more status to this work
    C. increase employees' feelings of security
    D. give employees greater motivation

4. An employee's performance has fallen below established minimum standards of quantity and quality.
The threat of monetary or other disciplinary action as a device for improving this employee's performance would PROBABLY be acceptable and most effective

    A. only if applied as soon as the performance fell below standard
    B. only after more constructive techniques have failed
    C. at any time provided the employee understands that the punishment will be carried out
    D. at no time

5. A supervisor must, on short notice, ask his staff to work overtime.
Of the following, a technique that is MOST likely to win their willing cooperation would be to

    A. explain that occasional overtime is part of the job requirement
    B. explain that they will be doing him a personal favor which he will appreciate very much
    C. explain why the overtime is necessary
    D. promise them that they can take the extra time off in the near future

1.____

2.____

3.____

4.____

5.____

6. On checking a completed work assignment of an employee, the supervisor finds that the work was not done correctly because the employee had not understood his instructions. Of the following, the BEST way to prevent repetition of this situation next time is for the supervisor to

    A. ask the employee whether he fully understood the instructions and tell him to ask questions in the future whenever anything is unclear
    B. ask the employee to repeat the instructions given and test his understanding with several key questions
    C. give the instructions a second time, emphasizing the more complicated aspects of the job
    D. give work instructions in writing

6.____

7. If, as a supervisor, you find yourself pressured for time to handle all of your job responsibilities, the one of the following tasks which it would be MOST appropriate for you to delegate to a subordinate is

    A. attending a staff conference of unit supervisors to discuss the implementation of a new departmental policy
    B. making staff work assignments
    C. interviewing a new employee
    D. checking work of certain employees for accuracy

7.____

8. Suppose you are unavoidably late for work one morning. When you arrive at 10 o'clock, you find there are several matters demanding your attention.
Which one of the following matters should you handle LAST?

    A. A visitor who had a 9:30 appointment with you has been waiting to see you since 9 o'clock
    B. An employee on an assignment which should have been completed that morning is absent, and the work will have to be reassigned
    C. Several letters which you dictated at the end of the previous day have been typed and are on your desk for signature and mailing
    D. Your superior called asking you to get certain information for him when you come in and to call him back

8.____

9. Suppose that you have assigned a typist to type a report containing considerable statistical and tabular material and have given her specific instructions as to how this material is to be laid out on each page. When she returns the completed report, you find that it was not prepared according to your instructions, but you may possibly be able to use it the way it was typed. When you question her, she states that she thought her layout was better, but you were unavailable for consultation when she began the work.
Of the following, the BEST action for you to take is to

    A. criticize her for not doing the work according to your instructions
    B. have her retype the report
    C. praise her for her work but tell her she could have waited until she could consult you
    D. praise her for using initiative

9.____

10. Of the following, the MOST effective way for a supervisor to correct poor working habits of an employee which result in low and poor quality output is to give the employee

10.____

8

A. additional training
B. less demanding assignments until his work improves
C. continuous supervision
D. more severe criticism

11. Of the following, the BEST way for a supervisor to teach an employee how to do a new and somewhat complicated job is to   11._____

   A. assign him to observe another employee who is already skilled in this work and instruct him to consult this employee if he has any questions
   B. explain to him how to do it, then demonstrate how it is done, then observe and correct the employee as he does it, then follow up
   C. give him a written, detailed, step-by-step explanation of how to do the job and instruct him to ask questions if anything is unclear when he does the work
   D. teach him the easiest part of the job first, then the other parts one at a time, in order of their difficulty, as the employee masters the easier parts

12. After an employee has completed telling his supervisor about a grievance against a co-worker, the supervisor tells the employee that he will take action to remove the cause of the grievance.   12._____
The action of the supervisor was

   A. *good* because ill feeling between subordinates interferes with proper performance
   B. *poor* because the supervisor should give both employees time to *cool off*
   C. *good* because grievances that appear petty to the supervisor are important to subordinates
   D. *poor* because the supervisor should tell the employee that he will investigate the matter before he comes to any conclusion

13. During work on an important project, one employee in a secretarial pool turns in several pages of typed copy, one page of which contains several errors.   13._____
Of these four comments which her supervisor might possibly make, which one would be MOST constructive?

   A. "You did such a poor job on this; I'll have to have it done over."
   B. "You will have to do better more consistently than this if you want to be in charge of a secretarial pool yourself someday."
   C. "How come you made so many mistakes here? Your other pages were all right."
   D. "If my boss saw this, he'd be very displeased with you."

14. A supervisor has general supervision over a large, complex project with many employees. The work is subdivided among small units of employees, each with a senior clerk or senior stenographer in charge. At a staff meeting, after all work assignments have been made, the supervisor tells all the employees that they are to take orders only from their immediate supervisor and instructs them to let him know if any one else tries to give them orders.   14._____
This instruction by the supervisor is

   A. *good* because it may prevent the issuance of orders by unauthorized persons which would interfere with the accomplishment of the assignment
   B. *poor* because employees should be instructed to take up such problems with their immediate supervisor

C. *good* because orders issued by immediate supervisors would be precise and directly related to the tasks of the assignments while those issued by others would not be

D. *poor* because it places upon all employees a responsibility which should not normally be theirs

15. A supervisor who is to direct a team of senior clerks and clerks and senior stenographers and stenographers in a complex project calls them together beforehand to inform them of the tasks each employee will perform on this job. Of the following, the CHIEF value of this action by the supervisor is that each member of this team will be able to

    A. work independently in the absence of the supervisor
    B. understand what he will do and how this will fit into the total picture
    C. share in the process of decision-making as an equal participant
    D. judge how well the plans for this assignment have been made

15.____

16. A supervisor who has both younger and older employees under his supervision may sometimes find that employee absenteeism seriously interferes with accomplishment of goals.
Studies of such employee absenteeism have shown that the absences of employees

    A. under 35 years of age are usually unexpected and the absences of employees over 45 years of age are usually unnecessary
    B. of all age groups show the same characteristics as to length of absence
    C. under 35 years of age are for frequent, short periods while the absences of employees over 45 years of age are less frequent but of longer duration
    D. under 35 years of age are for periods of long duration and the absences of employees over 45 years of age are for periods of short duration

16.____

17. Suppose you have a long-standing procedure for getting a certain job done by your subordinates that is apparently a good one. Changes in some steps of the procedure are made from time to time to handle special problems that come up.
For you to review this procedure periodically is desirable MAINLY because

    A. the system is working well
    B. checking routines periodically is a supervisor's chief responsibility
    C. subordinates may be confused as to how the procedure operates as a result of the changes made
    D. it is necessary to determine whether the procedure has become outdated or is in need of improvement

17.____

18. In conducting an interview, the BEST types of questions with which to begin the interview are those which the person interviewed is _____ to answer.

    A. willing and able   B. willing but unable
    C. able to but unwilling   D. unable and unwilling

18.____

19. In order to determine accurately a child's age, it is BEST for an interviewer to rely on

    A. the child's grade in school   B. what the mother says
    C. birth records   D. a library card

19.____

20. In his first interview with a new employee, it would be LEAST appropriate for a unit supervisor to

    A. find out the employee's preference for the several types of jobs to which he is able to assign him
    B. determine whether the employee will make good promotion material
    C. inform the employee of what his basic job responsibilities will be
    D. inquire about the employee's education and previous employment

20.____

21. If an interviewer takes care to phrase his questions carefully and precisely, the result will MOST probably be that

    A. he will be able to determine whether the person interviewed is being truthful
    B. the free flow of the interview will be lost
    C. he will get the information he wants
    D. he will ask stereotyped questions and narrow the scope of the interview

21.____

22. When, during an interview, is the person interviewed LEAST likely to be cautious about what he tells the interviewer?

    A. Shortly after the beginning when the questions normally suggest pleasant associations to the person interviewed
    B. As long as the interviewer keeps his questions to the point
    C. At the point where the person interviewed gains a clear insight into the area being discussed
    D. When the interview appears formally ended and goodbyes are being said

22.____

23. In an interview held for the purpose of getting information from the person interviewed, it is sometimes desirable for the interviewer to repeat the answer he has received to a question.
For the interviewer to rephrase such an answer in his own words is good practice MAINLY because it

    A. gives the interviewer time to make up his next question
    B. gives the person interviewed a chance to correct any possible misunderstanding
    C. gives the person interviewed the feeling that the interviewer considers his answer important
    D. prevents the person interviewed from changing his answer

23.____

24. There are several methods of formulating questions during an interview. The particular method used should be adapted to the interview problems presented by the person being questioned.
Of the following methods of formulating questions during an interview, the ACCEPTABLE one is for the interviewer to ask questions which

    A. incorporate several items in order to allow a cooperative interviewee freedom to organize his statements
    B. are ambiguous in order to foil a distrustful interviewee
    C. suggest the correct answer in order to assist an interviewee who appears confused
    D. would help an otherwise unresponsive interviewee to become more responsive

24.____

25. For an interviewer to permit the person being interviewed to read the data the interviewer   25.____
writes as he records the person's responses on a routine departmental form is

    A. *desirable* because it serves to assure the person interviewed that his responses
    are being recorded accurately
    B. *undesirable* because it prevents the interviewer from clarifying uncertain points by
    asking additional questions
    C. *desirable* because it makes the time that the person interviewed must wait while
    the answer is written seem shorter
    D. *undesirable* because it destroys the confidentiality of the interview

26. Suppose that a stranger enters the office you are in charge of and asks for the address   26.____
and telephone number of one of your employees.
Of the following, it would be BEST for you to

    A. find out why he needs the information and release it if his reason is a good one
    B. explain that you are not permitted to release such information to unauthorized per-
    sons
    C. give him the information but tell him it must be kept confidential
    D. ask him to leave the office immediately

27. A member of the public approaches an employee who is at work at his desk. The   27.____
employee cannot interrupt his work in order to take care of this person.
Of the following, the BEST and MOST courteous way of handling this situation is for
the employee to

    A. avoid looking up from his work until he is finished with what he is doing
    B. tell this person that he will not be able to take care of him for quite a while
    C. refer the individual to another employee who can take care of him right away
    D. chat with the individual while he continues with his work

28. You answer a phone call from a citizen who urgently needs certain information you do not   28.____
have, but you think you know who may have it. He is angry because he has already been
switched to two different offices.
Of the following, it would be BEST for you to

    A. give him the phone number of the person you think may have the information he
    wants, but explain you are not sure
    B. tell him you regret you cannot help him because you are not sure who can give him
    the information
    C. advise him that the best way he can be sure of getting the information he wants is
    to write a letter to the agency
    D. get the phone number where he can be reached and tell him you will try to get the
    information he wants and will call him back later

29. Persons who have business with an agency often complain about the *red tape* which   29.____
complicates or slows up what they are trying to accomplish.
As a supervisor of a unit which deals with the public, the LEAST effective of the following actions which you could take to counteract this feeling on the part of a person who
has business with your office is to

    A. assure him that your office will make every effort to take care of his matter as fast
    as possible
    B. tell him that because of the volume of work in your agency he must be patient with
    red tape

    C.   give him a reasonable date by which action on the matter he is concerned about will be completed and tell him to call you if he hasn't heard by then

    D.   give him an understanding of why the procedures he must comply with are necessary

30.   If a receptionist is sorting letters at her desk and a caller appears to make an inquiry, the receptionist should   30._____

    A.   ask the caller to have a seat and wait
    B.   speak to the caller while continuing the sorting, looking up occasionally
    C.   stop what she is doing and give undivided attention to the caller
    D.   continue with the sorting until a logical break in the work is reached, then answer any inquiries

31.   To avoid cutting off parts of letters when using an automatic letter opener, it is BEST to   31._____

    A.   arrange all of the letters so that the addresses are right side up
    B.   hold the envelopes up to the light to make sure their contents have not settled to the side that is to be opened
    C.   strike the envelopes against a table or desk top several times so that the contents of all the envelopes settle to one side
    D.   check the enclosures periodically to make sure that the machine has not been cutting into them

32.   Requests to repair office equipment which appears to be unsafe should be given priority MAINLY because if repairs are delayed   32._____

    A.   there may be injuries to staff
    B.   there may be further deterioration of the equipment
    C.   work flow may be interrupted
    D.   the cost of repair may increase

33.   Of the following types of documents, it is MOST important to retain and file   33._____

    A.   working drafts of reports that have been submitted in final form
    B.   copies of letters of good will which conveyed a message that could not be handled by phone
    C.   interoffice orders for materials which have been received and verified
    D.   interoffice memoranda regarding the routing of standard forms

34.   Of the following, the BEST reason for discarding certain material from office files would be that the   34._____

    A.   files are crowded
    B.   material in the files is old
    C.   material duplicates information obtainable from other sources in the files
    D.   material is referred to most often by employees in an adjoining office

35.   Of the following, the BEST reason for setting up a partitioned work area for the typists in your office is that   35._____

    A.   an uninterrupted flow of work among the typists will be possible
    B.   complaints about ventilation and lighting will be reduced
    C.   the first-line supervisor will have more direct control over the typists
    D.   the noise of the typewriters will be less disturbing to other workers

36. Of the following, the MAIN factor contributing to the expense of maintaining an office pro-   36.____
cedure manual would be the

    A. infrequent use of the manual   B. need to revise it regularly
    C. cost of looseleaf binders   D. high cost of printing

37. From the viewpoint of use of a typewriter to fill in a form, the MOST important design fac-   37.____
tor to consider is

    A. standard spacing   B. box headings
    C. serial numbering   D. vertical guide lines

38. Out-of-date and seldom used records should be removed PERIODICALLY from the files   38.____
because

    A. overall responsibility for records will be transferred to the person in charge of the
central storage files
    B. duplicate copies of every record are not needed
    C. valuable filing space will be regained and the time needed to find a current record
will be cut down
    D. worthwhile suggestions on improving the filing system will result whenever this is
done

39. In a certain office, file folders are constantly being removed from the files for use by   39.____
administrators. At the same time, new material is coming in to be filed in some of these
folders.
Of the following, the BEST way to avoid delays in filing of the new material and to keep
track of the removed folders is to

    A. keep a sheet listing all folders removed from the file, who has them, and a follow-up
date to check on their return; attach to this list new material received for filing
    B. put an *out* slip in the place of any file folder removed, telling what folder is missing,
date removed, and who has it; file new material received at front of files
    C. put a temporary *out* folder in place of the one removed, giving title or subject, date
removed, and who has it; put into this temporary folder any new material received
    D. keep a list of all folders removed and who has them; forward any new material
received for filing while a folder is out to the person who has it

40. Folders labeled *Miscellaneous* should be used in an alphabetic filing system MAINLY to   40.____

    A. provide quick access to recent material
    B. avoid setting up individual folders for all infrequent correspondents
    C. provide temporary storage for less important documents
    D. temporarily hold papers which will not fit into already crowded individual folders

41. Suppose that one of the office machines in your unit is badly in need of replacement.   41.____
Of the following, the MOST important reason for postponing immediate purchase of a
new machine would be that

    A. a later model of the machine is expected on the market in a few months
    B. the new machine is more expensive than the old machine
    C. the operator of the present machine will have to be instructed by the manufacturer
in the operation of the new machine
    D. the employee operating the old machine is not complaining

42. If the four steps listed below for processing records were given in logical sequence, the one that would be the THIRD step is: 42.____

    A. Coding the records, using a chart or classification system
    B. Inspecting the records to make sure they have been released for filing
    C. Preparing cross-reference sheets or cards
    D. Skimming the records to determine filing captions

43. The suggestion that memos or directives which circulate among subordinates be initialed by each employee is a   43.____

    A. *poor* one because, with modern copying machines, it should be possible to supply every subordinate with a copy of each message for his personal use
    B. *good* one because it relieves the supervisor of blame for the action of subordinates who have read and initialed the messages
    C. *poor* one because initialing the memo or directive is no guarantee that the subordinate has read the material
    D. *good* one because it can be used as a record by the supervisor to show that his subordinates have received the message and were responsible for reading it

44. Of the following, the MOST important reason for microfilming office records is to   44.____

    A. save storage space needed to keep records
    B. make it easier to get records when needed
    C. speed up the classification of information
    D. shorten the time which records must be kept

45. Your office filing cabinets have become so overcrowded that it is difficult to use the files. Of the following, the MOST desirable step for you to take FIRST to relieve this situation would be to   45.____

    A. assign your assistant to spend some time each day reviewing the material in the files and to give you his recommendations as to what material may be discarded
    B. discard all material which has been in the files more than a given number of years
    C. submit a request for additional filing cabinets in your next budget request
    D. transfer enough material to the central storage room of your agency to give you the amount of additional filing space needed

46. Of the following, the USUAL order of the subdivisions in a standard published report is: 46.____

    A. Table of contents, body of report, index, appendix
    B. Index, table of contents, body of report, appendix
    C. Index, body of report, table of contents, appendix
    D. Table of contents, body of report, appendix, index

47. The BEST type of pictorial illustration to show the approximate percentage breakdown of the titles of employees in a department would be the   47.____

    A. flow chart   B. bar graph
    C. organization chart   D. line graph

48. You are reviewing a draft, written by one of your subordinates, of a report that is to be distributed to every bureau and division of your department.
    Which one of the following would be the LEAST desirable characteristic of such a report?

    A. It gives information, explanations, conclusions, and recommendations for which purpose it was written.
    B. There is sufficient objective data presented to substantiate the conclusions reached and the recommendations made by the writer.
    C. The writing style and opinions of the writer are persuasive enough to win over to its conclusions those who read the report, although little data is given in support.
    D. It will be understood easily by the people to whom it will be distributed.

49. According to accepted practice, a business letter is addressed to an organization but marked for the attention of a specific individual whenever the sender wants

    A. only the person to whose attention the letter is sent to read the letter
    B. the letter to be opened and taken care of by someone else in the organization of the person for whose attention it is marked is away
    C. a reply only from the specific individual
    D. to improve the appearance and balance of the letter in cases where the company address is a long one

50. Which one of the following would be an ACCEPTABLE way to end a business letter?

    A. Hoping you will find this information useful, I remain
    B. Yours for continuing service
    C. I hope this letter gives you the information you need
    D. Trusting this gives you the information you desire, I am

---

KEY (CORRECT ANSWERS)

1.	A	11.	B	21.	C	31.	C	41.	A
2.	D	12.	D	22.	D	32.	A	42.	A
3.	A	13.	C	23.	B	33.	D	43.	D
4.	B	14.	B	24.	D	34.	C	44.	A
5.	C	15.	B	25.	A	35.	D	45.	A
6.	B	16.	C	26.	B	36.	B	46.	D
7.	D	17.	D	27.	C	37.	A	47.	B
8.	C	18.	A	28.	D	38.	C	48.	C
9.	A	19.	C	29.	B	39.	C	49.	B
10.	A	20.	B	30.	C	40.	B	50.	C

TEST 2

1. You are replying to a letter from an individual who asks for a pamphlet put out by your agency. The pamphlet is out of print. A new pamphlet with a different title, but dealing with the same subject, is available.
   Of the following, it would be BEST that your reply indicate that

   1.____

   A. you cannot send him the pamphlet he requested because it is out of print
   B. the pamphlet he requested is out of print, but he may be able to find it in the public library
   C. the pamphlet he requested is out of print, but you are sending him a copy of your agency's new pamphlet on the same subject
   D. since the pamphlet he requested is out of print, you would advise him to ask his friends or business acquaintances if they have a copy of it

2. An angry citizen sends a letter to your agency claiming that your office sent him the wrong form and complaining about the general inefficiency of city workers. Upon checking, you find that an incorrect form was indeed sent to this person.
   In reply, you should

   2.____

   A. admit the error, apologize briefly, and enclose the correct form
   B. send the citizen the correct form with a transmittal letter stating only that the form is enclosed
   C. send him the correct form without any comment
   D. advise the citizen that mistakes happen in every large organization and that you are enclosing the correct form

3. It has been suggested that the language level of a letter of reply written by a government employee be geared no higher than the probable educational level of the person to whom the letter is written.
   This suggestion is a

   3.____

   A. *good* one because it is easier for anyone to write letters simply, and this will make for a better reply
   B. *poor* one because it is not possible to judge, from one letter, the exact educational level of the writer
   C. *good* one because it will contribute to the recipient's comprehension of the contents of the letter
   D. *poor* one because the language should be at the simplest possible level so that anyone who reads the letter can understand it

4. Suppose that a large bureau has 187 employees. On a particular day, approximately 14% of these employees are not available for work because of absences due to vacation, illness, or other reasons. Of the remaining employees, 1/7 are assigned to a special project while the balance are assigned to the normal work of the bureau.
   The number of employees assigned to the normal work of the bureau on that day is

   4.____

   A. 112   B. 124   C. 138   D. 142

5. Suppose that you are in charge of a typing pool of 8 typists. Two typists type at the rate of 38 words per minute; three type at the rate of 40 words per minute; three type at the rate of 42 words per minute. The average typewritten page consists of 50 lines, 12 words per line. Each employee works from 9 to 5 with one hour off for lunch.
The total number of pages typed by this pool in one day is, on the average, CLOSEST to _____ pages.

   A. 205   B. 225   C. 250   D. 275

5.____

6. Suppose that part-time workers are paid $14.40 an hour, prorated to the nearest half hour, with pay guaranteed for a minimum of four hours if services are required for less than four hours. In one operation, part-time workers signed the time sheet as follows:

Worker	In	Out
A	8:00 A.M.	11:35 A.M.
B	8:30 A.M.	3:20 P.M.
C	7:55 A.M.	11:00 A.M.
D	8:30 A.M.	2:25 P.M.

How much would total payment to these part-time workers amount to for this operation, assuming that those who stayed after 12 Noon were not paid for one hour which they took off for lunch?

   A. $268.80   B. $273.60   C. $284.40   D. $297.60

6.____

7. He wanted to *ascertain* the facts before arriving at a conclusion.
The word *ascertain* means MOST NEARLY

   A. disprove   B. determine   C. convert   D. provide

7.____

8. Did the supervisor *assent* to her request for annual leave? The word *assent* means MOST NEARLY

   A. allude   B. protest   C. agree   D. refer

8.____

9. The new worker was fearful that the others would *rebuff* her.
The word *rebuff* means MOST NEARLY

   A. ignore   B. forget   C. copy   D. snub

9.____

10. The supervisor of that office does not *condone* lateness. The word *condone* means MOST NEARLY

   A. mind   B. excuse   C. punish   D. remember

10.____

11. Each employee was instructed to be as *concise* as possible when preparing a report.
The word *concise* means MOST NEARLY

   A. exact   B. sincere   C. flexible   D. brief

11.____

Questions 12-21.

DIRECTIONS: Below are 10 sentences numbered 12 to 21. Some of the sentences contain an error in spelling, word usage, or sentence structure, or punctuation. Some sentences are correct as they stand, although there may be other correct ways of expressing the same thought. All incorrect sentences contain only one error. Mark your answer to each question as follows:

A. if the sentence has an error in spelling
B. if the sentence has an error in punctuation or capitalization
C. if the sentence has an error in word usage or sentence structure
D. if the sentence is correct

12. Because the chairman failed to keep the participants from wandering off into irrelevant discussions, it was impossible to reach a consensus before the meeting was adjourned.   12._____

13. Certain employers have an unwritten rule that any applicant, who is over 55 years of age, is automatically excluded from consideration for any position whatsoever.   13._____

14. If the proposal to build schools in some new apartment buildings were to be accepted by the builders, one of the advantages that could be expected to result would be better communication between teachers and parents of schoolchildren.   14._____

15. In this instance, the manufacturer's violation of the law against deseptive packaging was discernible only to an experienced inspector.   15._____

16. The tenants' anger stemmed from the president's going to Washington to testify without consulting them first.   16._____

17. Did the president of this eminent banking company say; "We intend to hire and train a number of these disad-vantaged youths?"   17._____

18. In addition, today's confidential secretary must be knowledgable in many different areas: for example, she must know modern techniques for making travel arrangements for the executive.   18._____

19. To avoid further disruption of work in the offices, the protesters were forbidden from entering the building unless they had special passes.   19._____

20. A valuable secondary result of our training conferences is the opportunities afforded for management to observe the reactions of the participants.   20._____

21. Of the two proposals submitted by the committee, the first one is the best.   21._____

Questions 22-26.

DIRECTIONS: In Questions 22 through 26, choose the sentence which is BEST from the point of view of English usage suitable for a business letter or report.

22. A. It is the opinion of the Commissioners that programs which include the construction of cut-rate municipal garages in the central business district is inadvisable.   22._____
    B. Having reviewed the material submitted, the program for putting up cut-rate garages in the central business district seemed likely to cause traffic congestion.
    C. The Commissioners believe that putting up cut-rate municipal garages in the central business district is inadvisable.
    D. Making an effort to facilitate the cleaning of streets in the central business district, the building of cut-rate municipal garages presents the problem that it would encourage more motorists to come into the central city.

23. A. This letter, together with the reports, are to be sent to the principal.
    B. The reports, together with this letter, is to be sent to the principal.
    C. The reports and this letter is to be sent to the principal.
    D. This letter, together with the reports, is to be sent to the principal.

23.____

24. A. Each employee has to decide for themselves whether to take the examination.
    B. Each of the employees has to decide for himself whether to take the examination.
    C. Each of the employees has to decide for themselves whether to take the examination.
    D. Each of the employees have to decide for himself whether to take the examination.

24.____

25. A. The reason a new schedule is being prepared is that there has been a change in priorities.
    B. Because there has been a change in priorities is the reason why a new schedule is being made up.
    C. The reason why a new schedule is being made up is because there has been a change in priorities.
    D. Because of a change in priorities is the reason why a new schedule is being prepared.

25.____

26. A. The changes in procedure had an unfavorable affect upon the output of the unit.
    B. The increased output of the unit was largely due to the affect of the procedural changes.
    C. The changes in procedure had the effect of increasing the output of the unit.
    D. The increased output of the unit from the procedural changes were the effect.

26.____

Questions 27-33.

DIRECTIONS: Questions 27 through 33 are to be answered SOLELY on the basis of the information in the following extract, which is from a report prepared for Department X, which outlines the procedure to be followed in the case of transfers of employees.

Every transfer, regardless of the reason therefor, requires completion of the record of transfer, Form DT 411. To denote consent to the transfer, DT 411 should contain the signatures of the transferee and the personnel officer(s) concerned, except that, in the case of an involuntary transfer, the signatures of the transferee's present and prospective supervisors shall be entered in Boxes 8A and 8B, respectively, since the transferee does not consent. Only a permanent employee may request a transfer; in such cases, the employee's attendance record shall be duly considered with regard to absences, latenesses, and accrued overtime balances. In the case of an inter-district transfer, the employee's attendance record must be included in Section 8A of the transfer request, Form DT 410, by the personnel officer of the district from which the transfer is requested. The personnel officer of the district to which the employee requested transfer may refuse to accept accrued overtime balances in excess of ten days.

An employee on probation shall be eligible for transfer. If such employee is involuntarily transferred, he shall be credited for the period of time already served on probation. However, if such transfer is voluntary, the employee shall be required to serve the entire period of his probation in the new position. An employee who has occurred a disability which prevents him from performing his normal duties may be transferred during the period of such disability to other appropriate duties. A disability transfer requires the completion of either Form DT414 if the disability is job-connected, or Form DT 415 if it is not a job-connected disability. In either case, the personnel officer of the district from which the transfer is made signs in Box 6A of the first two copies and the personnel officer of the district to which the transfer is made signs in Box 6B of the last two copies; or, in the case of an intra-district disability transfer, the personnel officer must sign in Box 6A of the first two copies and Box 6B of the last two copies

27. When a personnel officer consents to an employee's request for transfer from his district, this procedure requires that the personnel officer sign Form(s)

   A. DT 411
   B. DT 410 and DT 411
   C. DT 411 and either Form DT 414 or DT 415
   D. DT 410 and DT 411, and either Form DT 414 or DT 415

27.____

28. With respect to the time record of an employee transferred against his wishes during his probationary period, this procedure requires that

   A. he serve the entire period of his probation in his present office
   B. he lose his accrued overtime balance
   C. his attendance record be considered with regard to absences and latenesses
   D. he be given credit for the period of time he has already served on probation

28.____

29. Assume you are a supervisor and an employee must be transferred into your office against his wishes.
   According to this procedure, the box you must sign on the record of transfer is

   A. 6A   B. 8A   C. 6B   D. 8B

29.____

30. Under this procedure, in the case of a disability transfer, when must Box 6A on Forms DT 414 and DT 415 be signed by the personnel officer of the district to which the transfer is being made?

   A. In all cases when either Form DT 414 or Form DT 415 is used
   B. In all cases when Form DT 414 is used and only under certain circumstances when Form DT 415 is used
   C. In all cases when Form DT 415 is used and only under certain circumstances when Form DT 414 is used
   D. Only under certain circumstances when either Form DT 414 or Form DT 415 is used

30.____

31. From the above passage, it may be inferred MOST correctly that the number of copies of Form DT 414 is

   A. no more than 2
   B. at least 3
   C. at least 5
   D. more than the number of copies of Form DT 415

31.____

32. A change in punctuation and capitalization only which would change one sentence into two and possibly contribute to somewhat greater ease of reading of this report extract would be MOST appropriate in the _____ sentence, _____ paragraph.

    A. 2nd; 1st
    C. next to the last; 2nd
    B. 3rd; 1st
    D. 2nd; 2nd

32.____

33. In the second paragraph, a word that is INCORRECTLY used is _____ in the _____ sentence.

    A. *shall;* 1st
    C. *occurred;* 4th
    B. *voluntary;* 3rd
    D. *intra-district;* last

33.____

Questions 34-38.

DIRECTIONS: Questions 34 through 38 are to be answered SOLELY on the basis of the information contained in the following passage.

Positive discipline minimizes the amount of personal supervision required and aids in the maintenance of standards. When a new employee has been properly introduced and carefully instructed, when he has come to know the supervisor and has confidence in the supervisor's ability to take care of him, when he willingly cooperates with the supervisor, that employee has been under positive discipline and can be put on his own to produce the quantity and quality of work desired. Negative discipline, the fear of transfer to a less desirable location, for example, to a limited extent may restrain certain individuals from overt violation of rules and regulations governing attendance and conduct which in governmental agencies are usually on at least an agency-wide basis. Negative discipline may prompt employees to perform according to certain rules to avoid a penalty such as, for example, docking for tardiness.

34. According to the above passage, it is reasonable to assume that in the area of discipline, the first-line supervisor in a governmental agency has GREATER scope for action in

    A. *positive* discipline because negative discipline is largely taken care of by agency rules and regulations
    B. *negative* discipline because rules and procedures are already fixed and the supervisor can rely on them
    C. *positive* discipline because the supervisor is in a position to recommend transfers
    D. *negative* discipline because positive discipline is reserved for people on a higher supervisory level

34.____

35. In order to maintain positive discipline of employees under his supervision, it is MOST important for a supervisor to

    A. assure each employee that he has nothing to worry about
    B. insist at the outset on complete cooperation from employees
    C. be sure that each employee is well trained in his job
    D. inform new employees of the penalties for not meeting standards

35.____

36. According to the above passage, a feature of negative discipline is that it

    A. may lower employee morale
    B. may restrain employees from disobeying the rules
    C. censures equal treatment of employees
    D. tends to create standards for quality of work

36.____

37. A REASONABLE conclusion based on the above passage is that positive discipline benefits a supervisor because   37.____

     A.   he can turn over orientation and supervision of a new employee to one of his subordinates
     B.   subordinates learn to cooperate with one another when working on an assignment
     C.   it is easier to administer
     D.   it cuts down, in the long run, on the amount of time the supervisor needs to spend on direct supervision

38. Based on the above passage, it is REASONABLE to assume that an important difference between positive discipline and negative discipline is that positive discipline   38.____

     A.   is concerned with the quality of work and negative discipline with the quantity of work
     B.   leads to a more desirable basis for motivation of the employee
     C.   is more likely to be concerned with agency rules and regulations
     D.   uses fear while negative discipline uses penalties to prod employees to adequate performance

Questions 39-50.

DIRECTIONS: Questions 39 through 50 are to be answered on the basis of the information given in the graph and chart below.

ENROLLMENT IN POSTGRADUATE STUDIES

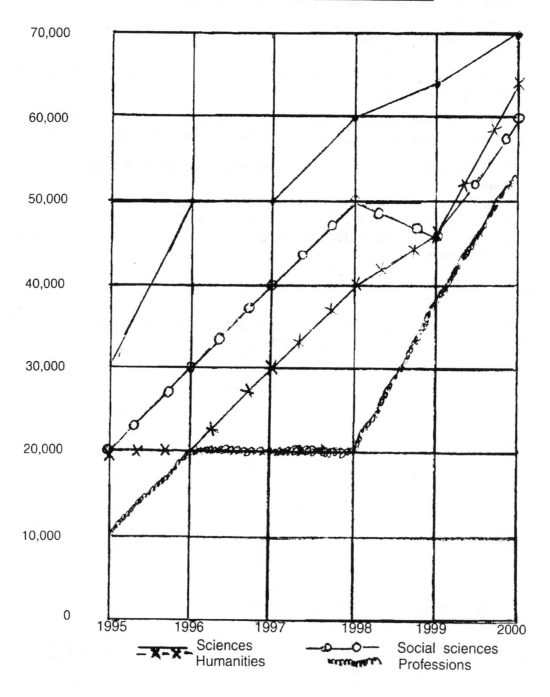

ENROLLMENT IN POSTGRADUATE STUDIES

Fields	Subdivisions	1999	2000
Sciences	Math	10,000	12,000
	Physical science	22,000	24,000
	Behavioral science	32,000	35,000
Humanities	Literature	26,000	34,000
	Philosophy	6,000	8,000
	Religion	4,000	6,000
	Arts	10,000	16,000
Social sciences	History	36,000	46,000
	Sociology	8,000	14.000
Professions	Law	2,000	2,000
	Medicine	6,000	8,000
	Business	30,000	44,000

39. The number of students enrolled in the social sciences and in the humanities was the same in _____ and _____.   39._____

    A. 1997; 1999   B. 1995; 1999
    C. 1999; 2000   D. 1996; 1999

40. A comparison of the enrollment of students in the various postgraduate studies shows that in every year from 1995 through 2000, there were more students enrolled in the _____ than in the _____.   40._____

    A. professions; sciences
    B. humanities; professions
    C. social sciences; professions
    D. humanities; sciences

41. The number of students enrolled in the humanities was GREATER than the number of students enrolled in the professions by the same amount in _____ of the years.   41._____

    A. two   B. three   C. four   D. five

42. The one field of postgraduate study to show a decrease in enrollment in one year compared to the year immediately preceding is   42._____

    A. humanities   B. sciences
    C. professions   D. social sciences

43. If the proportion of arts students to all humanities students was the same in 1997 as in 2000, then the number of arts students in 1997 was   43._____

    A. 7,500   B. 13,000   C. 15,000   D. 5,000

44. In which field of postgraduate study did enrollment INCREASE by 20 percent from 1997 to 1998?   44._____

    A. Humanities   B. Professions
    C. Sciences   D. Social sciences

45. The GREATEST increase in overall enrollment took place between   45._____

    A. 1995 and 1996   B. 1997 and 1998
    C. 1998 and 1999   D. 1999 and 2000

46. Between 1997 and 2000, the combined enrollment of the sciences and social sciences increased by   46.___

    A. 40,000   B. 48,000   C. 50,000   D. 54,000

47. If the enrollment in the social sciences had decreased from 1999 to 2000 at the same rate as from 1998 to 1999, then the social science enrollment in 2000 would have differed from the humanities enrollment in 2000 *MOST* NEARLY by   47.___

    A. 6,000   B. 8,000   C. 12,000   D. 22,000

48. In the humanities, the GREATEST percentage increase in enrollment from 1999 to 2000 was in   48.___

    A. literature   B. philosophy
    C. religion   D. arts

49. If the proportion of behavioral science students to the total number of students in the sciences was the same in 1996 as in 1999, then the increase in behavioral science enrollment from 1996 to 2000 was   49.___

    A. 5,000   B. 7,000   C. 10,000   D. 14,000

50. If enrollment in the professions increased at the same rate from 2000 to 2001 as from 1999 to 2000, the enrollment in the professions in 2001 would be MOST NEARLY   50.___

    A. 85,000   B. 75,000   C. 60,000   D. 55,000

KEY (CORRECT ANSWERS)

1. C	11. D	21. C	31. B	41. B
2. A	12. C	22. C	32. B	42. D
3. C	13. B	23. D	33. C	43. A
4. C	14. D	24. B	34. A	44. C
5. B	15. A	25. A	35. C	45. D
6. B	16. D	26. C	36. B	46. A
7. B	17. B	27. A	37. D	47. D
8. C	18. A	28. D	38. B	48. D
9. D	19. C	29. D	39. B	49. C
10. B	20. D	30. D	40. C	50. B

EXAMINATION SECTION
TEST 1

DIRECTIONS: Each question or incomplete statement is followed by several suggested answers or completions. Select the one that BEST answers the question or completes the statement. *PRINT THE LETTER OF THE CORRECT ANSWER IN THE SPACE AT THE RIGHT.*

1. Suppose you have received dictation of several letters and have been given no specific instructions as to the order in which the material should be transcribed. So far as you can see, all of the letters are equally important. Which of the following is BEST to do?

    A. Transcribe the letters in the order in which they were dictated to you.
    B. Ask a more experienced co-worker for her opinion as to the order of transcription.
    C. Use your own judgment as to the order in which you should transcribe the letters.
    D. Ask your supervisor if he wishes you to type the letters in a particular order.

1.____

2. Suppose you are in a unit which has many incoming calls from the public. Your supervisor has given you the job of training newly appointed typists in techniques for answering the telephone.
Of the following, which telephone response should be taught as the FIRST one to give upon picking up the telephone?

    A. Good morning. Who's calling, please?
    B. Who's this. Miss Smith speaking.
    C. Miss Smith. Who is this?
    D. Payroll Division. Miss Smith speaking.

2.____

3. You are in an office of 7 people. A woman calls your office, identifies herself as a client, and asks to speak to your supervisor, who is on another phone.
What should you do in this situation? Ask her

    A. to hold until your supervisor is off the line
    B. to call back in ten minutes when you expect your supervisor to be free
    C. what she wants, to see if you or someone else can help her
    D. what she wants and, if you cannot help her, hang us

3.____

4. As the supervisor of a unit of stenographers, you have given a new employee an assignment which can easily be completed by, and which is needed by, the end of the day. She indicates some anxiety and says that she is not sure she can complete it in time. The other employees are very busy and unable to help.
What should you do?

    A. Assign the stenographer to another task and finish the assignment yourself.
    B. Ask a supervisor from another unit if he could assign one of his workers to help your new stenographer.
    C. Tell the stenographer that right now is the time to conquer her anxiety by doing the job assigned to her.
    D. Review the assignment with the stenographer, check her progress, and be ready to help her when needed.

4.____

5. You supervise a stenographer who is writing many personal letters during work time while many of her assignments are not yet done.
    What should you do FIRST?

    A. Tell your supervisor that the stenographer needs more work since she is doing personal letters on the job.
    B. Make the stenographer stop personal work by telling her you will inform your supervisor unless she stops.
    C. Let the stenographer know that it is not proper to use government time for such personal projects.
    D. Give the stenographer enough work to keep her so busy that she won't be able to do personal work.

5.____

6. Suppose a stenographer working at an agency with equipment for transferring calls receives an outside call from someone who has reached the wrong extension. The stenographer knows the correct extension.
    The BEST thing for her to do in this case would be to

    A. signal the operator and tell him the extension to which to transfer the call
    B. give the caller the correct extension and offer to have him transferred to the correct extension
    C. give the person the correct extension and tell him to hang up and dial again
    D. tell the person he has reached the wrong extension and have him dial the operator

6.____

7. The supervisor in your office appears to be *dropping hints* about the condition of your desk. You feel that he may consider your desk somewhat sloppy.
    Which is the BEST way to handle this?

    A. Wait until your supervisor directly mentions your desk to you and then clean up.
    B. Straighten up your desk so that it can't be considered sloppy, and see if this stops the hints.
    C. Do nothing. Force your supervisor, by ignoring his hints, to stop *dropping the hints*.
    D. Tell the supervisor you have caught his hints and that now you would like him to speak his mind.

7.____

8. The instrument that should be used to write on a stencil is a

    A. stylus   B. ballpoint pen
    C. paper clip   D. pencil

8.____

9. A supervisor orienting a new stenographer advised her to be sure to note down in her notebook the date on which she took each piece of dictation. She told the stenographer to put the date on the same page as the dictated material.
    Which is the MOST important reason for dating the steno notebook? To

    A. know what date to put on the letters or reports the stenographer transcribes
    B. refer to these notes at a later date if necessary
    C. separate the letters from reports when transcribing them
    D. match incoming related correspondence to the material the stenographer transcribes

9.____

28

10. Assume you are in an office which uses a subject filing system. You find that frequently a letter to be filed involves two or three subjects.
In filing such a letter, it is MOST important to

    A. file it under the subject that is mentioned first in the letter
    B. prepare cross-references for the subjects covered in the letter
    C. list all subjects involved on the label of the file folder
    D. code the letter to show the main subject and its subdivisions

10.____

11. In addressing a letter to A.J. Brown, a commissioner in a governmental agency, the salutation that is considered MOST correct is:

    A. Ms. or Mr. Brown: B. Dear Commissioner Brown:
    C. My dear Sir or Madam: D. Commissioner Brown:

11.____

12. An office of a public agency frequently may need a number of copies of reports, forms, bulletins, letters, memos, and other kinds of written communications.
The particular type of duplicating process used to reproduce these copies does NOT usually depend on the

    A. quality of work produced
    B. number of copies required
    C. cost of duplication
    D. persons receiving the materials

12.____

13. A stenographer is transcribing a draft of a report from her notes. As soon as she transcribes a page of notes from her steno pad, she puts a line through that page. The MAIN reason for this procedure is that it

    A. prevents grammatical errors in the report
    B. prevents leaving out or repeating part of her notes
    C. prevents making typographical errors from her notes
    D. helps her to keep a count of the amount of work done

13.____

14. The MOST frequently used filing system in ordinary office practice is the _____ system.

    A. alphabetic   B. numeric
    C. geographic   D. subject

14.____

15. Your supervisor requests that you sign his name to, and mail, a letter he has dictated because he must leave to attend an important meeting.
In carrying out his request, you should remember to

    A. sign your full name and title below the signature
    B. imitate your superior's handwriting as closely as possible
    C. type *Dictated but not read* in the lower left hand corner
    D. add your initials next to or under the signature

15.____

16. Suppose a man speaking on the phone to you is having great difficulty making himself understood. He seems to be able to speak only in slang and cannot express himself easily.
What is the BEST thing to do to make sure you understand what he is saying?

16.____

A. Listen carefully, speak in your normal voice, and answer his questions as clearly as possible.
B. Use the same slang expressions and manner in which he speaks. This will give him confidence.
C. Let your irritation show in your voice so that he will *drop* his slang and speak more sensibly.
D. Ask your supervisor to answer his questions because the man's language is hard to understand.

17. There are few employees who do not seek meaning and some sort of challenge in their jobs.
Which of the following actions taken by a supervisor would BEST help to meet these needs?

    A. Constantly reminding subordinates of the agency's high work expectations.
    B. Explaining to subordinates how their work is related to that of other workers and how it contributes to agency objectives.
    C. Telling employees that the longer the time needed to perform a job, the more important the job is.
    D. Making it a policy to give each employee work which is slightly more difficult than his last assignment, but to explain such work carefully.

17.____

18. The one of the following over which a unit supervisor has the LEAST control is the _____ his unit.

    A. quality of the work done in
    B. nature of the work handled in
    C. morale of workers in
    D. increasing efficiency of

18.____

19. Suppose that you have received a note from an important official in your department commending the work of a unit of stenographers under your supervision.
Of the following, the BEST action for you to take is to

    A. withhold the note for possible use at a time when the morale of the unit appears to be declining
    B. show the note only to the better members of your staff as a reward for their good work
    C. show the note only to the poorer members of your staff as a stimulus for better work
    D. post the note conspicuously so that it can be seen by all members of your staff

19.____

20. If you find that one of your subordinates is becoming apathetic towards his work, you should

    A. prefer charges against him
    B. change the type of work
    C. request his transfer
    D. advise him to take a medical examination to check his health

20.____

21. Suppose that a new stenographer has been assigned to the unit which you supervise. To give this stenographer a brief picture of the functioning of your unit in the entire department would be

21.____

A. *commendable* because she will probably be able to perform her work with more understanding
B. *undesirable* because such action will probably serve only to confuse her
C. *commendable* because, if transferred, she would probably be able to work efficiently without additional training
D. *undesirable* because in-service training has been demonstrated to be less efficient than on-the-job training

22. Written instructions to a subordinate are of value because they   22.____

   A. can be kept up-to-date   B. encourage initiative
   C. make a job seem easier   D. are an aid in training

23. Suppose that you have assigned a task to a stenographer under your supervision and   23.____
    have given appropriate instructions. After a reasonable period, you check her work and
    find that one specific aspect of her work is consistently incorrect.
    Of the following, the BEST action for you to take is to

   A. determine whether the stenographer has correctly understood instructions concerning the aspect of the work not being done correctly
   B. assign the task to a more competent stenographer
   C. wait for the stenographer to commit a more flagrant error before taking up the matter with her
   D. indicate to the stenographer that you are dissatisfied with her work and wait to see whether she is sufficiently intelligent to correct her own mistakes

24. If you wanted to check on the accuracy of the filing in your unit, you would   24.____

   A. check all the files thoroughly at regular intervals
   B. watch the clerks while they are filing
   C. glance through filed papers at random
   D. inspect thoroughly a small section of the files selected at random

25. In making job assignments to his subordinates, a supervisor should follow the principle   25.____
    that each individual GENERALLY is capable of

   A. performing one type of work well and less capable of performing other types well
   B. learning to perform a wide variety of different types of work
   C. performing best the type of work in which he has had least experience
   D. learning to perform any type of work in which he is given training

KEY (CORRECT ANSWERS)

1.	D		11.	B
2.	D		12.	D
3.	C		13.	B
4.	D		14.	A
5.	C		15.	D
6.	B		16.	A
7.	B		17.	C
8.	A		18.	B
9.	B		19.	D
10.	B		20.	B

21.	A
22.	D
23.	A
24.	D
25.	B

———

TEST 2

DIRECTIONS: Each question or incomplete statement is followed by several suggested answers or completions. Select the one that BEST answers the question or completes the statement. *PRINT THE LETTER OF THE CORRECT ANSWER IN THE SPACE AT THE RIGHT.*

Questions 1-8.

DIRECTIONS: Questions 1 through 8 are to be answered on the basis of the RULES FOR ALPHABETICAL FILING given below. Read these rules carefully before answering the questions.

RULES FOR ALPHABETICAL FILING

Names of People

1.   The names of people are filed in strict alphabetical order, first according to the last name, then according to first name or initial, and finally according to middle name or initial. For example: George Allen comes before Edward Bell, and Leonard P. Reston comes before Lucille Reston.

2.   When last names are the same, for example, A. Green and Agnes Green, the one with the initial comes before the one with the name written out when the first initials are identical.

3.   When first and last names are alike and the middle name is given, for example, John David Doe and John Devoe Doe, the names should be filed in alphabetical order of the middle names.

4.   When first and last names are the same, a name without a middle initial comes before one with a middle name or initial. For example: John Doe comes before John A. Doe and John Alan Doe.

5.   When first and last names are the same, a name with a middle initial comes before one with a middle name beginning with the same initial. For example: Jack R. Hertz comes before Jack Richard Hertz.

6.   Prefixes such as De, O', Mac, Mc, and Van are filed as written and are treated as part of the names to which they are connected. For example: Robert O'Dea is filed before David Olsen.

7.   Abbreviated names are treated as if they were spelled out. For example: Chas. is filed as Charles, and Thos. is filed as Thomas.

8.   Titles and designations such as Dr., Mr., and Prof, are disregarded in filing.

Names of Organizations

1.   The names of business organizations are filed according to the order in which each word in the name appears. When an organization name bears the name of a person, it is filed according to the rules for filing names of people as given above. For example: William Smith Service Co. comes before Television Distributors, Inc.

2.   Where bureau, board, office, or department appears as the first part of the title of a governmental agency, that agency should be filed under the word in the title expressing the chief function of the agency. For example: Bureau of the Budget would be filed as if written Budget, (Bureau of the). The Department of Personnel would be filed as if written Personnel, (Department of).

3.   When the following words are part of an organization, they are disregarded: the, of, and.

4.   When there are numbers in a name, they are treated as if they were spelled out. For example: 10th Street Bootery is filed as Tenth Street Bootery.

Each of questions 1 through 8 contains four names numbered from I through IV, but not necessarily numbered in correct filing order. Answer each question by choosing the letter corresponding to the CORRECT filing order of the four names in accordance with the above rules.

Sample Question:

   I.   Robert J. Smith
   II. R. Jeffrey Smith
   III. Dr. A. Smythe
   IV. Allen R. Smithers

   A. I, II, III, IV   B. III, I, II, IV
   C. II, I, IV, III   D. III, II, I, IV

Since the correct filing order, in accordance with the above rules, is II, I, IV, III, the CORRECT answer is C.

1.   I.   J. Chester VanClief   1.____
     II. John C. VanClief
     III. J. VanCleve
     III. Mary L. Vance
     The CORRECT answer is:

   A. IV, III, I, II   B. IV, III, II, I
   C. III, I, II, IV   D. III, IV, I, II

2.   I.   Community Development Agency   2.____
     II. Department of Social Services
     III. Board of Estimate
     IV. Bureau of Gas and Electricity
     The CORRECT answer is:

A. III, IV, I, II   B. I, II, IV, III
C. II, I, III, IV   D. I, III, IV, II

3.   I.   Dr. Chas. K. Dahlman   3.____
      II.   F. & A. Delivery Service
     III.   Department of Water Supply
     IV.   Demano Men's Custom Tailors
     The CORRECT answer is:

A. I, II, III, IV   B. I, IV, II, III
C. IV, I, II, III   D. IV, I, III, II

4.   I.   48th Street Theater   4.____
      II.   Fourteenth Street Day Care Center
     III.   Professor A. Cartwright
     IV.   Albert F. McCarthy
     The CORRECT answer is:

A. IV, II, I, III   B. IV, III, I, II
C. III, II, I, IV   D. III, I, II, IV

5.   I.   Frances D'Arcy   5.____
      II.   Mario L. DelAmato
     III.   William R. Diamond
     IV.   Robert J. DuBarry
     The CORRECT answer is:

A. I, II, IV, III   B. II, I, III, IV
C. I, II, III, IV   D. II, I, IV, III

6.   I.   Evelyn H. D'Amelio   6.____
      II.   Jane R. Bailey
     III.   J. Robert Bailey
     IV.   Frank Baily
     The CORRECT answer is:

A. I, II, III, IV   B. I, III, II, IV
C. II, III, IV, I   D. III, II, IV, I

7.   I.   Department of Markets   7.____
      II.   Bureau of Handicapped Children
     III.   Housing Authority Administration Building
     IV.   Board of Pharmacy
     The CORRECT answer is:

A. II, I, III, IV   B. I, II, IV, III
C. I, II, III, IV   D. III, II, I, IV

8.   I.   William A. Shea Stadium   8.____
      II.   Rapid Speed Taxi Co.
     III.   Harry Stampler's Rotisserie
     IV.   Wilhelm Albert Shea
     The CORRECT answer is:

A. II, III, IV, I   B. IV, I, III, II
C. II, IV, I, III   D. III, IV, I, II

Questions 9-16.

DIRECTIONS: The employee identification codes in Column I begin and end with a capital letter and have an eight-digit number in between. In Questions 9 through 16,
employee identification codes in Column I are to be arranged according to the
following rules:

First: Arrange in alphabetical order according to the first letter.

Second: When two or more employee identification codes have the same first let
ter, arrange in alphabetical order according to the last letter.

Third: When two or more employee codes have the same first and last letters, arrange
in numerical order, beginning with the lowest number.

The employee identification codes in Column I are numbered 1 through 5 in the order in
which they are listed. In Column II, the numbers 1 through 5 are arranged in four different
ways to show different arrangements of the corresponding employee identification numbers.
Choose the answer in Column II in which the employee identification numbers are arranged
according to the above rules.

Sample Question;

	Column I		Column II				
1.	E75044127B	A.	4,	1,	3,	2,	5
2.	B96399104A	B.	4,	1,	2,	3,	5
3.	B93939086A	C.	4,	3,	2,	5,	1
4.	B47064465H	D.	3,	2,	5,	4,	1
5.	B99040922A						

In the sample question, the four employee identification codes starting with B should be
put before the employee identification code starting with E. The employee identification codes
starting with B and ending with A should be put before the employee identification codes
starting with B and ending with H. The three employee identification codes starting with B and
ending with A should be listed in numerical order, beginning with the lowest number. The correct way to arrange the employee identification codes, therefore, is 3, 2, 5, 4, 1, shown below.

3.   B93939086A
2.   B96399104A
5.   B99040922A
4.   B47064465H
1.   E75044127B

Therefore, the answer to the sample question is D.

	Column I		Column II	

9.	1. G42786441J	A. 2, 5, 4, 3, 1	9._____
	2. H45665413J	B. 5, 4, 1, 3, 2	
	3. G43117690J	C. 4, 5, 1, 3, 2	
	4. G43546698I	D. 1, 3, 5, 4, 2	
	5. G41679942I		

10.	1. S44556178T	A. 1, 3, 5, 2, 4	10._____
	2. T43457169T	B. 4, 3, 5, 2, 1	
	3. S53321176T	C. 5, 3, 1, 2, 4	
	4. T53317998S	D. 5, 1, 3, 4, 2	
	5. S67673942S		

11.	1. R63394217D	A. 5, 4, 2, 3, 1	11._____
	2. R63931247D	B. 1, 5, 3, 2, 4	
	3. R53931247D	C. 5, 3, 1, 2, 4	
	4. R66874239D	D. 5, 1, 2, 3, 4	
	5. R46799366D		

12.	1. A35671968B	A. 3, 2, 1, 4, 5	12._____
	2. A35421794C	B. 2, 3, 1, 5, 4	
	3. A35466987B	C. 1, 3 , 2, 4, 5	
	4. C10435779A	D. 3, 1, 2, 4, 5	
	5. C00634779B		

13.	1. I99746426Q	A. 2, 1, 3, 5, 4	13._____
	2. I10445311Q	B. 5, 4, 2, 1, 3	
	3. J63749877P	C. 4, 5, 3, 2, 1	
	4. J03421739Q	D. 2, 1, 4, 5, 3	
	5. J00765311Q		

14.	1. M33964217N	A. 4, 1, 5, 2, 3	14._____
	2. N33942770N	B. 5, 1, 4, 3, 2	
	3. N06155881M	C. 4, 1, 5, 3, 2	
	4. M00433669M	D. 1, 4, 5, 2, 3	
	5. M79034577N		

15.	1. D77643905C	A. 1, 2, 5, 3, 4	15._____
	2. D44106788C	B. 5, 3, 2, 1, 4	
	3. D13976022F	C. 2, 1, 5, 3, 4	
	4. D97655430E	D. 2, 1, 4, 5, 3	
	5. D00439776F		

16.	1. W22746920A	A. 2, 1, 3, 4, 5	16._____
	2. W22743720A	B. 2, 1, 5, 3, 4	
	3. W32987655A	C. 1, 2, 3, 4, 5	
	4. W43298765A	D. 1, 2, 5, 3, 4	
	5. W30987433A		

Questions 17-22.

DIRECTIONS: Questions 17 through 22 are to be answered on the basis of the information given in the chart below. This chart shows the results of a study made of the tasks performed by a stenographer during one day. Included in the chart are the time at which she started a certain task and, under the particular task heading, the amount of time, in minutes, she took to complete the task, and explanations of telephone calls and miscellaneous activities.

NOTE: The time spent at lunch should not be included in any of your calculations.

PAMELA JOB STUDY

NAME: Pamela Donald   DATE: 9/26
JOB TITLE: Stenographer
DIVISION: Stenographic Pool

Time of Start of Task	TASKS PERFORMED						Explanations of Telephone Calls and Miscellaneous Activities
	Taking Dictation	Typing	Filing	Telephone Work	Handling Mail	Misc. Activities	
9:00					22		
9:22						13	Picking up supplies
9:35						15	Cleaning typewriter
9:50	11						
10:01		30					
10:31				8			Call to Agency A
10:39	12						
10:51			10				
11:01				7			Call from Agency B
11:08		30					
11:38	10						
11:48				12			Call from Agency C
12:00	L U N C H						
1:00					28		
1:28	13						
1:41		32					
2:13				12			Call to Agency B
X			15				
Y		50					
3:30	10						
3:40			21				
4:01				9			Call from Agency A
4:10	35						
4:45		9					
4:54						6	Cleaning up desk

Sample Question;

The total amount of time spent on miscellaneous activities in the morning is exactly equal to the total amount of time spent

    A.   filing in the morning
    B.   handling mail in the afternoon
    C.   miscellaneous activities in the afternoon
    D.   handling mail in the morning

Explanation of answer to sample question:

    The total amount of time spent on miscellaneous activities in the morning equals 28 minutes (13 minutes for picking up supplies plus 15 minutes for cleaning the typewriter); and since it takes 28 minutes to handle mail in the afternoon, the answer is B.

17.   The time labeled Y at which the stenographer started a typing assignment was   17._____

    A.   2:15   B.   2:25   C.   2:40   D.   2:50

18.   The ratio of time spent on all incoming calls to time spent on all outgoing calls for the day   18._____
    was

    A.   5:7   B.   5:12   C.   7:5   D.   7:12

19.   Of the following combinations of tasks, which ones take up exactly 80% of the total time   19._____
    spent on *Tasks Performed* during the day?

    A.   Typing, filing, telephone work, and handling mail
    B.   Taking dictation, filing, and miscellaneous activities
    C.   Taking dictation, typing, handling mail, and miscellaneous activities
    D.   Taking dictation, typing, filing, and telephone work

20.   The total amount of time spent transcribing or typing work is how much more than the   20._____
    total amount of time spent in taking dictation?

    A.   55 minutes   B.   1 hour
    C.   1 hour 10 minutes   D.   1 hour 25 minutes

21.   The GREATEST number of shifts in activities occurred between the times of   21._____

    A.   9:00 A.M. and 10:31 A.M.
    B.   9:35 A.M. and 11:01 A.M.
    C.   10:31 A.M. and 12:00 Noon
    D.   3:30 P.M. and 5:00 P.M.

22.   The total amount of time spent on taking dictation in the morning plus the total amount of   22._____
    time spent on filing in the afternoon is exactly equal to the total amount of time spent on

    A.   typing in the afternoon minus the total amount of time spent on telephone work in
         the afternoon
    B.   typing in the morning plus the total amount of time spent on miscellaneous activities in the afternoon
    C.   dictation in the afternoon plus the total amount of time spent on filing in the morning

D. typing in the afternoon minus the total amount of time spent on handling mail in the morning

Questions 23-30.

DIRECTIONS: Each of Questions 23 through 30 consists of a set of letters and numbers. For each question, pick as your answer from the column to the right the choice which has ONLY numbers and letters that are in the question you are answering.

Sample Question:

B-9-P-H-2-Z-N-8-4-M

    A. B-4-C-3-H-9
    B. 4-H-P-8-6-N
    C. P-2-Z-8-M-9
    D. 4-B-N-5-E-2

Choice C is the correct answer because P, 2, Z, 8, M, 9 are in the sample question. All the other choices have at least one letter or number that is not in the question.

Questions 23 through 26 are based on Column I.
Questions 27 through 30 are based on Column II.

Column I

23. X-8-3-I-H-9-4-G-P-U	A. I-G-W-8-2-1	23._____
24. 4-1-2-X-U-B-9-H-7-3	B. U-3-G-9-P-8	24._____
25. U-I-G-2-5-4-W-P-3-8	C. 3-G-I-4-8-U	25._____
26. 3-H-7-G-4-5-I-U-8	D. 9-X-4-7-2-H	26._____

Column II

27. L-2-9-Z-R-8-Q-Y-5-7	A. 8-R-N-3-T-Z	27._____
28. J-L-9-N-Y-8-5-Q-Z-2	B. 2-L-R-5-7-Q	28._____
29. T-Y-8-3-J-Q-2-N-R-Z	C. J-2-8-Z-Y-5	29._____
30. 8-Z-7-T-N-L-1-E-R-3	D. Z-8-9-3-L-5	30._____

KEY (CORRECT ANSWERS)

1.	A		16.	B
2.	D		17.	C
3.	B		18.	C
4.	D		19.	D
5.	C		20.	B
6.	D		21.	C
7.	D		22.	D
8.	C		23.	B
9.	B		24.	D
10.	D		25.	C
11.	C		26.	C
12.	D		27.	B
13.	A		28.	C
14.	C		29.	A
15.	D		30.	A

TEST 3

DIRECTIONS: Each question or incomplete statement is followed by several suggested answers or completions. Select the one that BEST answers the question or completes the statement. *PRINT THE LETTER OF THE CORRECT ANSWER IN THE SPACE AT THE RIGHT.*

Questions 1-6.

DIRECTIONS: In Questions 1 through 6, only one of the sentences lettered A, B, C, or D is grammatically correct. Pick as your answer the sentence that is CORRECT from the point of view of grammar when used in formal correspondence.

1.   A.   There is four tests left.   1._____
     B.   The number of tests left are four.
     C.   There are four tests left.
     D.   Four of the tests remains.

2.   A.   Each of the applicants takes a test.   2._____
     B.   Each of the applicants take a test.
     C.   Each of the applicants take tests.
     D.   Each of the applicants have taken tests.

3.   A.   The applicant, not the examiners, are ready.   3._____
     B.   The applicants, not the examiner, is ready.
     C.   The applicants, not the examiner, are ready.
     D.   The applicant, not the examiner, are ready.

4.   A.   You will not progress except you practice.   4._____
     B.   You will not progress without you practicing.
     C.   You will not progress unless you practice.
     D.   You will not progress provided you do not practice.

5.   A.   Neither the director or the employees will be at the office tomorrow.   5._____
     B.   Neither the director nor the employees will be at the office tomorrow.
     C.   Neither the director, or the secretary nor the other employees will be at the office tomorrow.
     D.   Neither the director, the secretary or the other employees will be at the office tomorrow.

6.   A.   In my absence he and her will have to finish the assignment.   6._____
     B.   In my absence,he and she will have to finish the assignment.
     C.   In my absence she and him, they will have to finish the assignment.
     D.   In my absence he and her both will have to finish the assignment.

Questions 7-12.

DIRECTIONS: Questions 7 through 12 consist of a sentence lacking certain needed punctuation. Pick as your answer the description of punctuation which will CORRECTLY complete the sentence.

7. If you take the time to keep up your daily correspondence you will no doubt be most efficient.
   Comma(s)   7.____

    A. only after *doubt*
    B. only after *correspondence*
    C. after *correspondence, will,* and *be*
    D. after *if, correspondence,* and *will*

8. Because he did not send the application soon enough he did not receive the up to date copy of the book. Comma(s)   8.____

    A. after *application* and *enough,* and quotation marks before *up* and after *date*
    B. after *application* and *enough,* and hyphens between *to* and *date*
    C. after *enough,* and hyphens between *up* and *to* and between *to* and *date*
    D. after *application,* and quotation marks before *up* and after *date*

9. The coordinator requested from the department the following items a letter each week summarizing progress personal forms and completed applications for tests.   9.____

    A. Commas after *items* and *completed*
    B. Semi-colon after *items* and *progress,* comma after *forms*
    C. Colon after *items,* commas after *progress* and *forms*
    D. Colon after *items,* commas after *forms* and *applications*

10. The supervisor asked Who will attend the conference next month   10.____

    A. Comma after *asked,* period after *month*
    B. Period after *asked,* question mark after *month*
    C. Comma after *asked,* quotation marks before *Who,* quotation marks after *month,* and question mark after the quotation marks
    D. Comma after *asked,* quotation marks before *Who,* question mark after *month,* and quotation marks after the question mark

11. When the statistics are collected we will forward the results to you as soon as possible.   11.____
    Comma(s) after

    A. *you*
    B. *forward* and *you*
    C. *collected, results,* and *you*
    D. *collected*

12. The ecology of our environment is concerned with mans pollution of the atmosphere.   12.____

    A. Comma after *ecology*
    B. Apostrophe after *n* and before *s* in *mans*
    C. Commas after *ecology* and *environment*
    D. Apostrophe after *s* in *mans*

Questions 13-18.

DIRECTIONS: Each of Questions 13 through 18 consists of three words. In each question, one of the words may be spelled incorrectly or all three words may be spelled correctly. If one of the words in a question is spelled incorrectly, indicate in the space at the right the letter preceding the word which is spelled incorrectly. If all three words are spelled correctly, print in the space at the right the letter D.

13. A. sincerely   B. affectionately   C. truly   13.____

14. A. excellant   B. verify   C. important   14.____

15. A. error   B. quality   C. enviroment   15.____

16. A. exercise   B. advance   C. pressure   16.____

17. A. citizen   B. expence   C. memory   17.____

18. A. flexable   B. focus   C. forward   18.____

19. A senior stenographer earned $40,200 a year and had 4.5% state tax withheld for the year 2016.   19.____
If she was paid every two weeks, the amount of state tax that was taken out of each of her paychecks, based on a 52-week year, was MOST NEARLY

   A. $62.76   B. $64.98   C. $69.54   D. $73.98

20. Two stenographers have been assigned to address 750 envelopes. One stenographer addresses twice as many envelopes per hour as the other stenographer.   20.____
If it takes five hours for them to complete the job, the rate of the slower stenographer is _____ envelopes per hour.

   A. 35   B. 50   C. 75   D. 100

21. Suppose that the postage rate for mailing single copies of a magazine to persons not included on a subscription list is 60 cents for the first two ounces of the single copy and 10 cents for each additional ounce.   21.____
If 19 copies of a magazine, each of which weighs eleven ounces, are mailed to 19 different people, the TOTAL postage cost of these magazines is

   A. $11.40   B. $13.30   C. $20.90   D. $28.50

22. A senior stenographer spends about 40 hours a month taking dictation. Of that time, 44% is spent taking minutes of meetings, 38% is spent taking dictation of lengthy reports, and the rest of the time is spent taking dictation of letters and memoranda.   22.____
How much MORE time is spent taking minutes of meetings than in taking dictation of letters and memoranda?
10 hours _____minutes

   A. 6   B. 16   C. 24   D. 40

23. In one week, a stenographer typed 65 letters. Forty letters had 4 copies on onion skin.   23.____
The rest had 3 copies on onion skin.
If the stenographer had 500 sheets of onion skin on hand at the beginning of the week
when she started typing the letters, how many sheets of onion skin did she have left at
the end of the week?

    A. 190   B. 235   C. 265   D. 305

24. An agency is planning to microfilm letters and other correspondence of the last five   24.____
years. The number of letter size documents that can be photographed on a 100-foot roll
of microfilm is 2,995. The agency estimates that it will need 240 feet of microfilm to do all
the pages of all of the letters.
How many pages of letter size documents can be photographed on this microfilm?

    A. 5,990   B. 6,786   C. 7,188   D. 7,985

25. In an agency, 2/3 of the total number of female stenographers and 1/2 of the total number   25.____
of male stenographers attended a general staff meeting.
If there are a total of 56 stenographers in the agency and 25% of them are male, the
number of female stenographers who attended the general staff meeting is

    A. 14   B. 28   C. 36   D. 42

26. A worker is currently earning $42,850 a year and pays $875 a month for rent. He   26.____
expects to get a raise that will enable him to move into an apartment where his rent will
be 25% of his new yearly salary.
If this new apartment is going to cost him $975 a month, what is the TOTAL amount of
raise that he expects to get?

    A. $1,200   B. $2,450   C. $3,950   D. $4,600

27. The tops of five desks in an office are to be covered with a scratch-resistant material.   27.____
Each desk top measures 60 inches by 36 inches.
How many square feet of material will be needed for the five desk tops?

    A. 15   B. 75   C. 96   D. 180

Questions 28-33.

DIRECTIONS: Questions 28 through 33 test how well you understand what you read. It will be
necessary for you to read carefully because your answers to these questions
should be based ONLY on the information given in the following passage.

        Years ago, senior stenographers needed to understand the basic operations of
data processing. On punched cards, magnetic tape or on other media, data was
recorded before being fed into the computer for processing. A machine such as the
keypunch was used to convert the data written on the source document into the coded
symbols on punched cards or tapes. After data was converted, it was verified to
guarantee absolute accuracy of conversion. In this manner, data became a permanent
record that can be read by electronic computers.

Today, senior stenographers enter similar data directly into computer systems using word-processing, spreadsheet, publishing and other types of software. Rather than concern themselves with symbols and conversions, stenographers can transcribe information in programs like Microsoft Word or Google Docs, and enter numerical information into Microsoft Excel, which can then create charts and formulas out of that basic data.

28. Of the following, the BEST title for the above passage is:　　　　　28.____

    A. THE STENOGRAPHER AS DATA PROCESSOR
    B. THE RELATION OF KEYPUNCHING TO STENOGRAPHY
    C. THE EVOLUTION OF DATA PROCESSING
    D. PERMANENT OFFICE RECORDS

29. According to the above passage, the role of the senior stenographer is different in the　　29.____
present day in that

    A. data can be entered directly into computer programs
    B. it requires knowledge of multiple methods of recording data
    C. ultimately, all data winds up being recorded on a computer
    D. stenographers must have an advanced understanding of software and programming

30. Based on the passage, which of the following is NOT an example of a task a senior　　30.____
stenographer would carry out today?

    A. Entering text into a pamphlet using publishing software
    B. Recording sales figures and sending them to a programmer for processing
    C. Recording purchasing data in an Excel spreadsheet
    D. Typing an orally dictated draft in a Word document

31. According to the above passage, computers are used MOST often to handle　　31.____

    A. management data
    B. problems of higher education
    C. the control of chemical processes
    D. payroll operations

32. Computer programming is taught in many colleges and business schools.　　32.____
The above passage IMPLIES that programmers in industry

    A. must have professional training
    B. need professional training to advance
    C. must have at least a college education to do adequate programming tasks
    D. do not need college education to do programming work

33. According to the above passage, data to be processed by computer should be　　33.____

    A. recent   B. complete   C. basic   D. verified

Questions 34-40.

DIRECTIONS: In each of the following groups of sentences, one of the four sentences is faulty in grammar, punctuation, or capitalization. Select the INCORRECT sentence in each case.

34.   A. If you had stood at home and done your homework, you would not have failed in arithmetic.   34.____
      B. Her affected manner annoyed every member of the audience.
      C. How will the new law affect our income taxes?
      D. The plants were not affected by the long, cold winter, but they succumbed to the drought of summer.

35.   A. He is one of the most able men who have been in the Senate.   35.____
      B. It is he who is to blame for the lamentable mistake.
      C. Haven't you a helpful suggestion to make at this time?
      D. The money was robbed from the blind man's cup.

36.   A. The amount of children in this school is steadily increasing.   36.____
      B. After taking an apple from the table, she went out to play.
      C. He borrowed a dollar from me.
      D. I had hoped my brother would arrive before me.

37.   A. Whom do you think I hear from every week?   37.____
      B. Who do you think is the right man for the job?
      C. Who do you think I found in the room?
      D. He is the man whom we considered a good candidate for the presidency.

38.   A. Quietly the puppy laid down before the fireplace.   38.____
      B. You have made your bed; now lie in it.
      C. I was badly sunburned because I had lain too long in the sun.
      D. I laid the doll on the bed and left the room.

39.   A. Sailing down the bay was a thrilling experience for me.   39.____
      B. He was not consulted about your joining the club.
      C. This story is different than the one I told you yesterday.
      D. There is no doubt about his being the best player.

40.   A. He maintains there is but one road to world peace.   40.____
      B. It is common knowledge that a child sees much he is not supposed to see.
      C. Much of the bitterness might have been avoided if arbitration had been resorted to earlier in the meeting.
      D. The man decided it would be advisable to marry a girl somewhat younger than him.

KEY (CORRECT ANSWERS)

1.	C	21.	D
2.	A	22.	C
3.	C	23.	C
4.	C	24.	C
5.	B	25.	B
6.	B	26.	C
7.	B	27.	B
8.	C	28.	C
9.	C	29.	A
10.	D	30.	B
11.	D	31.	A
12.	B	32.	D
13.	D	33.	D
14.	A	34.	A
15.	C	35.	D
16.	D	36.	A
17.	B	37.	C
18.	A	38.	A
19.	C	39.	C
20.	B	40.	D

EXAMINATION SECTION
TEST 1

DIRECTIONS: Each question or incomplete statement is followed by several suggested answers or completions. Select the one that BEST answers the question or completes the statement. *PRINT THE LETTER OF THE CORRECT ANSWER IN THE SPACE AT THE RIGHT.*

1. A supervisor may be required to help train a newly appointed clerk. Which of the following is LEAST important for a newly appointed clerk to know in order to perform his work efficiently?

   A. Acceptable ways of answering and recording telephone calls
   B. The number of files in the storage files unit
   C. The filing methods used by his unit
   D. Proper techniques for handling visitors

1._____

2. In your agency you have the responsibility of processing clients who have appointments with agency representatives. On a particularly busy day, a client comes to your desk and insists that she must see the person handling her case although she has no appointment.
   Under the circumstances, your FIRST action should be to

   A. show her the full appointment schedule
   B. give her an appointment for another day
   C. ask her to explain the urgency
   D. tell her to return later in the day

2._____

3. Which of the following practices is BEST for a supervisor to use when assigning work to his staff?

   A. Give workers with seniority the most difficult jobs
   B. Assign all unimportant work to the slower workers
   C. Permit each employee to pick the job he prefers
   D. Make assignments based on the workers' abilities

3._____

4. In which of the following instances is a supervisor MOST justified in giving commands to people under his supervision? When

   A. they delay in following instructions which have been given to them clearly
   B. they become relaxed and slow about work, and he wants to speed up their production
   C. he must direct them in an emergency situation
   D. he is instructing them on jobs that are unfamiliar to them

4._____

5. Which of the following supervisory actions or attitudes is MOST likely to result in getting subordinates to try to do as much work as possible for a supervisor?
   He

   A. shows that his most important interest is in schedules and production goals
   B. consistently pressures his staff to get the work out
   C. never fails to let them know he is in charge
   D. considers their abilities and needs while requiring that production goals be met

5._____

6. Assume that a supervisor has been explaining certain regulations to a new clerk under his supervision.
The MOST efficient way for the supervisor to make sure that the clerk has understood the explanation is to

   A. give him written materials on the regulations
   B. ask him if he has any further questions about the regulations
   C. ask him specific questions based on what has just been explained to him
   D. watch the way he handles a situation involving these regulations

6.____

7. One of your unit clerks has been assigned to work for a Mr. Jones in another office for several days. At the end of the first day, Mr. Jones, saying the clerk was not satisfactory, asks that she not be assigned to him again. This clerk is one of your most dependable workers, and no previous complaints about her work have come to you from any other outside assignments.
To get to the root of this situation, your FIRST action should be to

   A. ask Mr. Jones to explain in what way her work was unsatisfactory
   B. ask the clerk what she did that Mr. Jones considered unsatisfactory
   C. check with supervisors for whom she previously worked to see if your own rating of her is in error
   D. tell Mr. Jones to pick the clerk he would prefer to have work for him the next time

7.____

8. A senior typist, still on probation, is instructed to type, as quickly as possible, one section of a draft of a long, complex report. Her part must be typed and readable before another part of the report can be written. Asked when she can have the report ready, she gives her supervisor an estimate of a day longer than she knows it will actually take. She then finishes the job a day sooner than the date given her supervisor.
The judgment shown by the senior typist in giving an overestimate of time in a situation like this is, in general,

   A. *good* because it prevents the supervisor from thinking she works slowly
   B. *good* because it keeps unrealistic supervisors from expecting too much
   C. *bad* because she should have used the time left to further check and proofread her work
   D. *bad* because schedules and plans for other parts of the project may have been based on her false estimate

8.____

9. Suppose a new clerk, still on probation, is placed under your supervision and refuses to do a job you ask him to do. What is the FIRST thing you should do?

   A. Explain that you are the supervisor and he must follow your instructions.
   B. Tell him he may be suspended if he refuses.
   C. Ask someone else to do the job and rate him accordingly.
   D. Ask for his reason for objecting to the request.

9.____

10. As a supervisor of a small group of people, you have blamed worker A for something that you later find out was really done by worker B.
The BEST thing for you to do now would be to

10.____

A. say nothing to worker A but criticize worker B for his mistake while worker A is near so that A will realize that you know who made the mistake
B. speak to each worker separately, apologize to worker A for your mistake, and discuss worker B's mistake with him
C. bring both workers together, apologize to worker A for your mistake, and discuss worker B's mistake with him
D. say nothing now but be careful about mixing up worker A with worker B in the future

11. You have just learned one of your staff is grumbling that she thinks you are not pleased with her work. As far as you're concerned, this isn't true at all. In fact, you've paid no particular attention to this worker lately because you've been very busy. You have just finished preparing an important report and *breaking in* a new clerk.
Under the circumstances, the BEST thing to do is

A. ignore her; after all, it's just a figment of her imagination
B. discuss the matter with her now to try to find out and eliminate the cause of this problem
C. tell her not to worry about it; you haven't had time to think about her work
D. make a note to meet with her at a later date in order to straighten out the situation

11.____

12. A most important job of a supervisor is to positively motivate employees to increase their work production. Which of the following LEAST indicates that a group of workers has been positively motivated?

A. Their work output becomes constant and stable.
B. Their cooperation at work becomes greater.
C. They begin to show pride in the product of their work.
D. They show increased interest in their work.

12.____

13. Which of the following traits would be LEAST important in considering a person for a merit increase?

A. Punctuality
C. High rate of production
B. Using initiative successfully
D. Resourcefulness

13.____

14. Of the following, the action LEAST likely to gain a supervisor the cooperation of his staff is for him to

A. give each person consideration as an individual
B. be as objective as possible when evaluating work performance
C. rotate the least popular assignments
D. expect subordinates to be equally competent

14.____

15. It has been said that, for the supervisor, nothing can beat the *face-to-face* communication of talking to one subordinate at a time.
This method is, however, LEAST appropriate to use when the

A. supervisor is explaining a change in general office procedure
B. subject is of personal importance
C. supervisor is conducting a yearly performance evaluation of all employees
D. supervisor must talk to some of his employees concerning their poor attendance and punctuality

15.____

16. While you are on the telephone answering a question about your agency, a visitor comes to your desk and starts to ask you a question. There is no emergency or urgency in either situation, that of the phone call or that of answering the visitor's question.
In this case, you should

    A. continue to answer the person on the telephone until you are finished and then tell the visitor you are sorry to have kept him waiting
    B. excuse yourself to the person on the telephone and tell the visitor that you will be with him as soon as you have finished on the phone
    C. explain to the person on the telephone that you have a visitor and must shorten the conversation
    D. continue to answer the person on the phone while looking up occasionally at the visitor to let him know that you know he is waiting

17. While speaking on the telephone to someone who called, you are disconnected.
The FIRST thing you should do is

    A. hang up but try to keep your line free to receive the call back
    B. immediately get the dialtone and continually dial the person who called you until you reach him
    C. signal the switchboard operator and ask her to re-establish the connection
    D. dial *0* for Operator and explain that you were disconnected

18. The type of speech used by an office worker in telephone conversations greatly affects the communicator.
Of the following, the BEST way to express your ideas when telephoning is with a vocabulary that consists mainly of _____ words.

    A. formal, intellectual sounding
    B. often used colloquial
    C. technical, emphatic
    D. simple, descriptive

19. Suppose a clerk under your supervision has taken a personal phone call and is at the same time needed to answer a question regarding an assignment being handled by another member of your office. He appears confused as to what he should do. How should you instruct him later as to how to handle a similar situation?
You should tell him to

    A. tell the caller to hold on while he answers the question
    B. tell the caller to call back a little later
    C. return the call during an assigned break
    D. finish the conversation quickly and answer the question

20. You are asked to place a telephone call by your supervisor. When you place the call, you receive what appears to be a wrong number.
Of the following, you should FIRST

    A. check the number with your supervisor to see if the number he gave you is correct
    B. ask the person on the other end what his number is and who he is
    C. check with the person on the other end to see if the number you dialed is the number you received
    D. apologize to the person on the other end for disturbing him and hang up

16.____

17.____

18.____

19.____

20.____

Questions 21-30.

WORD MEANING

DIRECTIONS: Each Question 21 through 30 contains a word in capitals followed by four suggested meanings of the word. For each question, choose the BEST meaning
and write the letter of the best meaning in the space at the right.

21. ACCURATE   21.____

    A. correct   B. useful   C. afraid   D. careless

22. ALTER   22.____

    A. copy   B. change   C. repeat   D. agree

23. DOCUMENT   23.____

    A. outline   B. agreement   C. blueprint   D. record

24. INDICATE   24.____

    A. listen   B. show   C. guess   D. try

25. INVENTORY   25.____

    A. custom   B. discovery   C. warning   D. list

26. ISSUE   26.____

    A. annoy   B. use up   C. give out   D. gain

27. NOTIFY   27.____

    A. inform   B. promise   C. approve   D. strengthen

28. ROUTINE   28.____

    A. path   B. mistake   C. habit   D. journey

29. TERMINATE   29.____

    A. rest   B. start   C. deny   D. end

30. TRANSMIT   30.____

    A. put in   B. send   C. stop   D. go across

Questions 31-35.

READING COMPREHENSION

DIRECTIONS: Questions 31 through 35 test how well you understand what you read. It will be
necessary for you to read carefully because your answers to these questions
should be based SOLELY on the information given in the following paragraphs.

The recipient gains an impression of a typewritten letter before he begins to read the message. Factors which provide for a good first impression include margins and spacing that are visually pleasing, formal parts of the letter which are correctly placed according to the style of the letter, copy which is free of obvious erasures and over-strikes, and transcript that is even and clear. The problem for the typist is that of how to produce that first, positive impression of her work.

There are several general rules which a typist can follow when she wishes to prepare a properly spaced letter on a sheet of letterhead. Ordinarily, the width of a letter should not be less the four inches nor more than six inches. The side margins should also have a desirable relation to the bottom margin and the space between the letterhead and the body of the letter. Usually the most appealing arrangement is when the side margins are even and the bottom margin is slightly wider than the side margins. In some offices, however, standard line length is used for all business letters, and the secretary then varies the spacing between the date line and the inside address according to the length of the letter.

31. The BEST title for the above paragraphs would be: 31._____

    A. Writing Office Letters
    B. Making Good First Impressions
    C. Judging Well-Typed Letters
    D. Good Placing and Spacing for Office Letters

32. According to the above paragraphs, which of the following might be considered the way in which people very quickly judge the quality of work which has been typed? By 32._____

    A. measuring the margins to see if they are correct
    B. looking at the spacing and cleanliness of the typescript
    C. scanning the body of the letter for meaning
    D. reading the date line and address for errors

33. What, according to the above paragraphs, would be definitely UNDESIRABLE as the average line length of a typed letter? 33._____

    A. 4"   B. 5"   C. 6"   D. 7"

34. According to the above paragraphs, when the line length is kept standard, the secretary 34._____

    A. does not have to vary the spacing at all since this also is standard
    B. adjusts the spacing between the date line and inside address for different lengths of letters
    C. uses the longest line as a guideline for spacing between the date line and inside address
    D. varies the number of spaces between the lines

35. According to the above paragraphs, side margins are MOST pleasing when they 35._____

    A. are even and somewhat smaller than the bottom margin
    B. are slightly wider than the bottom margin
    C. vary with the length of the letter
    D. are figured independently from the letterhead and the body of the letter

Questions 36-40.

CODING

DIRECTIONS: Name of Applicant   H A N G S B R U K E
           Test Code   c o m p l e x i t y
           File Number   0 1 2 3 4 5 6 7 8 9

Assume that each of the above capital letters is the first letter of the name of an applicant, that the small letter directly beneath each capital letter is the test code for the applicant, and that the number directly beneath each code letter is the file number for the applicant.

In each of the following Questions 36 through 40, the test code letters and the file numbers in Columns 2 and 3 should correspond to the capital letters in Column 1. For each question, look at each Column carefully and mark your answer as follows:

If there is an error only in Column 2, mark your answer A.
If there is an error only in Column 3, mark your answer B.
If there is an error in both Columns 2 and 3, mark your answer C.
If both Columns 2 and 3 are correct, mark your answer D.

The following sample question is given to help you understand the procedure.

SAMPLE QUESTION

Column 1	Column 2	Column 3
AKEHN	otyci	18902

In Column 2, the final test code letter *i* should be *m*. Column 3 is correctly coded to Column 1. Since there is an error only in Column 2, the answer is A.

	Column 1	Column 2	Column 3	
36.	NEKKU	mytti	29987	36._____
37.	KRAEB	txlye	86095	37._____
38.	ENAUK	ymoit	92178	38._____
39.	REANA	xeomo	69121	39._____
40.	EKHSE	ytcxy	97049	40._____

Questions 41-50.

ARITHMETICAL REASONING

DIRECTIONS: Solve the following problems.

41. If a secretary answered 28 phone calls and typed the addresses for 112 credit statements in one morning, what is the RATIO of phone calls answered to credit statements typed for that period of time?   41._____

     A. 1:4   B. 1:7   C. 2:3   D. 3:5

42. According to a suggested filing system, no more than 10 folders should be filed behind   42.___
any one file guide, and from 15 to 25 file guides should be used in each file drawer for
easy finding and filing.
The MAXIMUM number of folders that a five-drawer file cabinet can hold to allow easy
finding and filing is

    A. 550   B. 750   C. 1,100   D. 1,250

43. An employee had a starting salary of $32,902. He received a salary increase at the end   43.___
of each year, and at the end of the seventh year, his salary was $36,738. What was his
AVERAGE annual increase in salary over these seven years?

    A. $510   B. $538   C. $548   D. $572

44. The 55 typists and 28 senior clerks in a certain agency were paid a total of $1,943,200 in   44.___
salaries for the year. If the average annual salary of a typist was $22,400, the AVERAGE
annual salary of a senior clerk was

    A. $25,400   B. $26,600   C. $26,800   D. $27,000

45. A typist has been given a three-page report to type. She has finished typing the first two   45.___
pages. The first page has 283 words, and the second page has 366 words.
If the total report consists of 954 words, how many words will she have to type on the
third page of the report?

    A. 202   B. 287   C. 305   D. 313

46. In one day, Clerk A processed 30% more forms than Clerk B, and Clerk C processed   46.___
11/4 as many forms as Clerk A.
If Clerk B processed 40 forms, how many MORE forms were processed by Clerk C
than Clerk B?

    A. 12   B. 13   C. 21   D. 25

47. A clerk who earns a gross salary of $452 every week has the following deductions taken   47.___
from her paycheck: 17 1/2% for City, State, Federal taxes, and for Social Security, $1.20
for health insurance, and $6.10 for union dues. The amount of her take-home pay is

    A. $286.40   B. $312.40   C. $331.60   D. $365.60

48. In 2006 an agency spent $200 to buy pencils at a cost of $1 a dozen.   48.___
If the agency used 3/4 of these pencils in 2006 and used the same number of pencils
in 2007, how many MORE pencils did it have to buy to have enough pencils for all of
2007?

    A. 1,200   B. 2,400   C. 3,600   D. 4,800

49. A clerk who worked in Agency X earned the following salaries: $30,070 the first year,   49.___
$30,500 the second year, and $30,960 the third year. Another clerk who worked in
Agency Y for three years earned $30,550 a year for two years and $30,724 the third year.
The DIFFERENCE between the average salaries received by both clerks over a three-
year period is

    A. $98   B. $102   C. $174   D. $282

50. An employee who works over 40 hours in any week receives overtime payment for the extra hours at time and one-half (1 1/2 times) his hourly rate of pay. An employee who earns $7.80 an hour works a total of 45 hours during a certain week.
His TOTAL pay for that week would be

    A. $312.00   B. $351.00   C. $370.50   D. $412.00

50.____

_____

KEY (CORRECT ANSWERS)

1.	B	11.	B	21.	A	31.	D	41.	A
2.	C	12.	A	22.	B	32.	B	42.	D
3.	D	13.	A	23.	D	33.	D	43.	C
4.	C	14.	D	24.	B	34.	B	44.	A
5.	D	15.	A	25.	D	35.	A	45.	C
6.	C	16.	B	26.	C	36.	B	46.	D
7.	A	17.	A	27.	A	37.	C	47.	D
8.	D	18.	D	28.	C	38.	D	48.	B
9.	D	19.	C	29.	D	39.	A	49.	A
10.	B	20.	C	30.	B	40.	C	50.	C

_____

TEST 2

DIRECTIONS: Each question or incomplete statement is followed by several suggested answers or completions. Select the one that BEST answers the question or completes the statement. *PRINT THE LETTER OF THE CORRECT ANSWER IN THE SPACE AT THE RIGHT.*

1. To tell a newly employed clerk to fill a top drawer of a four-drawer cabinet with heavy folders which will be often used and to keep lower drawers only partly filled is   1.___

    A. *good* because a tall person would have to bend unnecessarily if he had to use a lower drawer
    B. *bad* because the file cabinet may tip over when the top drawer is opened
    C. *good* because it is the most easily reachable drawer for the average person
    D. *bad* because a person bending down at another drawer may accidentally bang his head on the bottom of the drawer when he straightens up

2. If you have requisitioned a *ream* of paper in order to duplicate a single page office announcement, how many announcements can be printed from the one package of paper?   2.___

    A. 200   B. 500   C. 700   D. 1,000

3. In the operations of a government agency, a voucher is ORDINARILY used to   3.___

    A. refer someone to the agency for a position or assignment
    B. certify that an agency's records of financial transactions are accurate
    C. order payment from agency funds of a stated amount to an individual
    D. enter a statement of official opinion in the records of the agency

4. Of the following types of cards used in filing systems, the one which is generally MOST helpful in locating records which might be filed under more than one subject is the _____ card.   4.___

    A. cut   B. tickler
    C. cross-reference   D. visible index

5. The type of filing system in which one does NOT need to refer to a card index in order to find the folder is called   5.___

    A. alphabetic   B. geographic   C. subject   D. locational

6. Of the following, records management is LEAST concerned with   6.___

    A. the development of the best method for retrieving important information
    B. deciding what records should be kept
    C. deciding the number of appointments a client will need
    D. determining the types of folders to be used

7. If records are continually removed from a set of files without *charging* them to the borrower, the filing system will soon become ineffective.
    Of the following terms, the one which is NOT applied to a form used in a charge-out system is a   7.___

    A. requisition card   B. out-folder
    C. record retrieval form   D. substitution card

8. A new clerk has been told to put 500 cards in alphabetical order. Another clerk suggests that she divide the cards into four groups such as A to F, G to L, M to R, and S to Z, and then alphabetize these four smaller groups.
The suggested method is

    A. *poor* because the clerk will have to handle the sheets more than once and will waste time
    B. *good* because it saves time, is more accurate, and is less tiring
    C. *good* because she will not have to concentrate on it so much when it is in smaller groups
    D. *poor* because this method is much more tiring than straight alphabetizing

8.____

9. The term that describes the equipment attached to an office computer is

    A. interface   B. network   C. hardware   D. software

9.____

10. Suppose a clerk has been given pads of pre-printed forms to use when taking phone messages for others in her office. The clerk is then observed using scraps of paper and not the forms for writing her messages.
It should be explained that the BEST reason for using the forms is that

    A. they act as a checklist to make sure that the important information is taken
    B. she is expected to do her work in the same way as others in the office
    C. they make sure that unassigned paper is not wasted on phone messages
    D. learning to use these forms will help train her to use more difficult forms

10.____

11. Of the following, the one which is spelled incorrectly is

    A. alphabetization   B. reccommendation
    C. redaction   D. synergy

11.____

12. Of the following, the MAIN reason a stock clerk keeps a perpetual inventory of supplies in the storeroom is that such an inventory will

    A. eliminate the need for a physical inventory
    B. provide a continuous record of supplies on hand
    C. indicate whether a shipment of supplies is satisfactory
    D. dictate the terms of the purchase order

12.____

13. As a supervisor, you may be required to handle different types of correspondence.
Of the following types of letters, it would be MOST important to promptly seal which kind of letters?

    A. One marked *confidential*
    B. Those containing enclosures
    C. Any letter to be sent airmail
    D. Those in which carbons will be sent along with the original

13.____

14. While opening incoming mail, you notice that one letter indicates that an enclosure was to be included but, even after careful inspection, you are not able to find the information to which this refers.
Of the following, the thing that you should do FIRST is

14.____

A. replace the letter in its envelope and return it to the sender
B. file the letter until the sender's office mails the missing information
C. type out a letter to the sender informing them of their error
D. make a notation in the margin of the letter that the enclosure was omitted

15. You have been given a checklist and assigned the responsibility of inspecting certain equipment in the various offices of your agency.
Which of the following is the GREATEST advantage of the checklist?

15.___

A. It indicates which equipment is in greatest demand.
B. Each piece of equipment on the checklist will be checked only once.
C. It helps to insure that the equipment listed will not be overlooked.
D. The equipment listed suggests other equipment you should look for.

16. Your supervisor has asked you to locate a telephone number for an attorney named Jones, whose office is located at 311 Broadway and whose name is not already listed in your files.
The BEST method for finding the number would be for you to

16.___

A. call the information operator and have her get it for you
B. look in the alphabetical directory (white pages) under the name Jones at 311 Broadway
C. refer to the heading Attorney in the yellow pages for the name Jones at 311 Broadway
D. ask your supervisor who referred her to Mr. Jones, then call that person for the number

17. An example of material that should NOT be sent by first class mail is a

17.___

A. carbon copy of a letter   B. postcard
C. business reply card   D. large catalogue

18. Which of the following BEST describes *office work simplification?*

18.___

A. An attempt to increase the rate of production by speeding up the movements of employees
B. Eliminating wasteful steps in order to increase efficiency
C. Making jobs as easy as possible for employees so they will not be overworked
D. Eliminating all difficult tasks from an office and leaving only simple ones

19. The duties of a supervisor who is assigned the job of timekeeper may include all of the following EXCEPT

19.___

A. computing and recording regular hours worked each day in accordance with the normal work schedule
B. approving requests for vacation leave, sick leave, and annual leave
C. computing and recording overtime hours worked beyond the normal schedule
D. determining the total regular hours and total extra hours worked during the week

20. Suppose a clerk under your supervision accidentally opens a personal letter while handling office mail.
Under such circumstances, you should tell the clerk to put the letter back into the envelope and

20.___

A. take the letter to the person to whom it belongs and make sure he understands that the clerk did not read it
B. try to seal the envelope so it won't appear to have been opened
C. write on the envelope *Sorry - opened by mistake,* and put his initials on it
D. write on the envelope *Sorry - opened by mistake,* but not put his initials on it

Questions 21-25.

SPELLING

DIRECTIONS: Each Question 21 through 25 consists of three words. In each question, one of the words may be spelled incorrectly or all three may be spelled correctly. For each question, if one of the words is spelled incorrectly, write the letter of the incorrect word in the space at the right. If all three words are spelled correctly, write the letter D in the space at the right.

SAMPLE I: (A) guide   (B) departmint   (C) stranger

SAMPLE II: (A) comply   (B) valuable   (C) window

In the Sample Question I, *departmint* is incorrect.
It should be spelled *department.* Therefore, B is the
answer to Sample Question I.
In the Sample Question II, all three words are spelled correctly. Therefore, D is
the answer to Sample Question II.

21.	A. argument	B. reciept	C. complain	21._____
22.	A. sufficient	B. postpone	C. visible	22._____
23.	A. expirience	B. dissatisfy	C. alternate	23._____
24.	A. occurred	B. noticable	C. appendix	24._____
25.	A. anxious	B. guarantee	C. calender	25._____

Questions 26-30.

ENGLISH USAGE

DIRECTIONS: Each Question 26 through 30 contains a sentence. Read each sentence carefully to decide whether it is correct. Then, in the space at the right, mark your answer:
(A) if the sentence is incorrect because of bad grammar or sentence structure
(B) if the sentence is incorrect because of bad punctuation
(C) if the sentence is incorrect because of bad capitalization
(D) if the sentence is correct

Each incorrect sentence has only one type of error. Consider a sentence correct if it has no errors, although there may be other correct ways of saying the same thing.

SAMPLE QUESTION I: One of our clerks were promoted
yesterday.

The subject of this sentence is *one,* so the verb should be *was promoted* instead of *were promoted.* Since the sentence is incorrect because of bad grammar, the answer to Sample Question I is A.

SAMPLE QUESTION II: Between you and me, I would prefer
not going there.

Since this sentence is correct, the answer to Sample Question II is D.

26. The National alliance of Businessmen is trying to persuade private businesses to hire youth in the summertime.   26.___

27. The supervisor who is on vacation, is in charge of processing vouchers.   27.___

28. The activity of the committee at its conferences is always stimulating.   28.___

29. After checking the addresses again, the letters went to the mailroom.   29.___

30. The director, as well as the employees, are interested in sharing the dividends. 30.___

Questions 31-40.

FILING

DIRECTIONS: Each Question 31 through 40 contains four names. For each question, choose the name that should be FIRST if the four names are to be arranged in alphabetical order in accordance with the Rules for Alphabetical Filing given below. Read these rules carefully. Then, for each question, indicate in the correspondingly numbered space at the right the letter before the name that should be FIRST in alphabetical order.

RULES FOR ALPHABETICAL FILING

Names of People

(1) The names of people are filed in strict alphabetical order, first according to the last name, then according to first name or initial, and finally according to middle name or initial. For example: George Allen comes before Edward Bell, and Leonard P. Reston comes before Lucille B. Reston.

(2) When last names are the same, for example A. Green and Agnes Green, the one with the initial comes before the one with the name written out when the first initials are identical.

(3) When first and last names are alike and the middle name is given, for example John David Doe and John Devoe Doe, the names should be filed in the alphabetical order of the middle names.

(4) *When first and last names are the same, a name without a middle initial comes before one with a middle name or initial. For example: John Doe comes before both John A. Doe and John Alan Doe.*

(5) *When first and last names are the same, a name with a middle initial comes before one with a middle name beginning with the same initial. For example: Jack R. Herts comes before Jack Richard Hertz.*

(6) *Prefixes such as De, 0', Mac, Mc, and Van are filed as written and are treated as part of the names to which they are connected. For example: Robert O'Dea is filed before David Olsen.*

(7) *Abbreviated names are treated as if they were spelled out. For example: Chas. is filed as Charles and Thos. is filed as Thomas.*

(8) *Titles and designations such as Dr., Mr., and Prof, are disregarded in filing.*

Names of Organizations

(1) *The names of business organizations are filed according to the order in which each word in the name appears. When an organization name bears the name of a person, it is filed according to the rules for filing names of people as given above. For example: William Smith Service Co. comes before Television Distributors, Inc.*

(2) *Where bureau, board, office or department appears as the first part of the title of a governmental agency, that agency should be filed under the word in the title expressing the chief function of the agency. For example: Bureau of the Budget would be filed as if written Budget, (Bureau of the). The Department of Personnel would be filed as if written Personnel, (Department of).*

(3) *When the following words are part of an organization, they are disregarded: the, of, and.*

(4) *When there are numbers in a name, they are treated as if they were spelled out. For example: 10th Street Bootery is filed as Tenth Street Bootery.*

SAMPLE QUESTION: (A) Jane Earl   (2)
                  (B) James A. Earle   (4)
                  (C) James Earl   (1)
                  (D) J. Earle   (3)

The numbers in parentheses show the proper alphabetical order in which these names should be filed. Since the name that should be filed FIRST is James Earl, the answer to the sample question is C.

31. A. Majorca Leather Goods   31.____
     B. Robert Maiorca and Sons
     C. Maintenance Management Corp.
     D. Majestic Carpet Mills

32.   A. Municipal Telephone Service   32.___
      B. Municipal Reference Library
      C. Municipal Credit Union
      D. Municipal Broadcasting System

33.   A. Robert B. Pierce   B. R. Bruce Pierce   33.___
      C. Ronald Pierce   D. Robert Bruce Pierce

34.   A. Four Seasons Sports Club   34.___
      B. 14 Street Shopping Center
      C. Forty Thieves Restaurant
      D. 42nd St. Theaters

35.   A. Franco Franceschini   B. Amos Franchini   35.___
      C. Sandra Franceschia   D. Lilie Franchinesca

36.   A. Chas. A. Levine   B. Kurt Levene   36.___
      C. Charles Levine   D. Kurt E. Levene

37.   A. Prof. Geo. Kinkaid   B. Mr. Alan Kinkaid   37.___
      C. Dr. Albert A. Kinkade   D. Kincade Liquors Inc.

38.   A. Department of Public Events   38.___
      B. Office of the Public Administrator
      C. Queensborough Public Library
      D. Department of Public Health

39.   A. Martin Luther King, Jr. Towers   39.___
      B. Metro North Plaza
      C. Manhattanville Houses
      D. Marble Hill Houses

40.   A. Dr. Arthur Davids   40.___
      B. The David Check Cashing Service
      C. A.C. Davidsen
      D. Milton Davidoff

Questions 41-45.

READING COMPREHENSION

DIRECTIONS: Questions 41 through 45 test how well you understand what you read. It will be necessary for you to read carefully because your answers to these questions should be based SOLELY on the information given in the following paragraph.

Work standards presuppose an ability to measure work. Measurement in office management is needed for several reasons. First, it is necessary to evaluate the overall efficiency of the office itself. It is then essential to measure the efficiency of each particular section or unit and that of the individual worker. To plan and control the work of sections and units, one must have measurement. A program of measurement goes hand in hand with a program of standards. One can have measurement without standards, but one cannot have work standards without measurement. Providing data on amount of work done and time expended, measure-

ment does not deal with the amount of energy expended by an individual although in many cases such energy may be in direct proportion to work output. Usually from two-thirds to three-fourths of all work can be measured. However, less than two-thirds of all work is actually measured because measurement difficulties are encountered when office work is non-repetitive and irregular, or when it is primarily mental rather than manual. These obstacles are often used as excuses for non-measurement far more frequently than is justified.

41. According to the paragraph, an office manager cannot set work standards unless he can   41._____

    A. plan the amount of work to be done
    B. control the amount of work that is done
    C. estimate accurately the quantity of work done
    D. delegate the amount of work to be done to efficient workers

42. According to the paragraph, the type of office work that would be MOST difficult to measure would be   42._____

    A. checking warrants for accuracy of information
    B. recording payroll changes
    C. processing applications
    D. making up a new system of giving out supplies

43. According to the paragraph, the actual amount of work that is measured is _____ of all work.   43._____

    A. less than two-thirds
    B. two-thirds to three-fourths
    C. less than three-sixths
    D. more than three-fourths

44. Which of the following would be MOST difficult to determine by using measurement techniques?   44._____

    A. The amount of work that is accomplished during a certain period of time
    B. The amount of work that should be planned for a period of time
    C. How much time is needed to do a certain task
    D. The amount of incentive a person must have to do his job

45. The one of the following which is the MOST suitable title for the paragraph is: 45._____

    A. How Measurement of Office Efficiency Depends on Work Standards
    B. Using Measurement for Office Management and Efficiency
    C. Work Standards and the Efficiency of the Office Worker
    D. Managing the Office Using Measured Work Standards

Questions 46-50.

INTERPRETING STATISTICAL DATA

DIRECTIONS: Answer Questions 46 through 50 using the information given in the table below.

AGE COMPOSITION IN THE LABOR FORCE IN CITY A
(1990-2000)

	Age Group	1990	1995	2000
Men	14 - 24	8,430	10,900	14,340
	25 - 44	22,200	22,350	26,065
	45+	17,550	19,800	21,970
Women	14 - 24	4,450	6,915	7,680
	25 - 44	9,080	10,010	11,550
	45+	7,325	9,470	13,180

46. The GREATEST increase in the number of people in the labor force between 1990 and 1995 occurred among   46.___

    A. men between the ages of 14 and 24
    B. men age 45 and over
    C. women between the ages of 14 and 24
    D. women age 45 and over

47. If the total number of women of all ages in the labor force increases from 2000 to 2005 by the same number as it did from 1995 to 2000, the TOTAL number of women of all ages in the labor force in 2005 will be   47.___

    A. 27,425   B. 29,675   C. 37,525   D. 38,425

48. The total increase in numbers of women in the labor force from 1990 to 1995 differs from the total increase of men in the same years by being _____ than that of men.   48.___

    A. 770 less   B. 670 more   C. 770 more   D. 1,670 more

49. In the year 1990, the proportion of married women in each group was as follows: 1/5 of the women in the 14-24 age group, 1/4 of those in the 25-44 age group, and 2/5 of those 45 and over.
    How many married women were in the labor force in 1990?   49.___

    A. 4,625   B. 5,990   C. 6,090   D. 7,910

50. The 14-24 age group of men in the labor force from 1990 to 2000 increased by APPROXIMATELY   50.___

    A. 40%   B. 65%   C. 70%   D. 75%

KEY (CORRECT ANSWERS)

1. B	11. B	21. B	31. C	41. C
2. B	12. B	22. D	32. D	42. D
3. C	13. A	23. A	33. B	43. A
4. C	14. D	24. B	34. D	44. D
5. A	15. C	25. C	35. C	45. B
6. C	16. C	26. C	36. B	46. A
7. C	17. D	27. B	37. D	47. D
8. B	18. B	28. D	38. B	48. B
9. C	19. B	29. A	39. A	49. C
10. A	20. C	30. A	40. B	50. C

———

EXAMINATION SECTION
TEST 1

DIRECTIONS: Each question or incomplete statement is followed by several suggested answers or completions. Select the one that BEST answers the question or completes the statement. *PRINT THE LETTER OF THE CORRECT ANSWER IN THE SPACE AT THE RIGHT.*

1. A coworker has e-mailed a file containing a spreadsheet for your review. Which of the following programs will open the file?   1._____

    A. Adobe Reader
    B. Microsoft Excel
    C. Microsoft PowerPoint
    D. Adobe Illustrator

2. A report needs to be forwarded immediately to a supervisor in another office. Which of the following is the LEAST effective way of giving the supervisor the report?   2._____

    A. scanning the report and e-mailing the file
    B. faxing it to the supervisor's office
    C. uploading it to the office network and informing the supervisor
    D. waiting for the supervisor to come to your office and giving it to him/her then

3. Suppose your supervisor is on the telephone in his office and an applicant arrives for a scheduled interview with him.
Of the following, the BEST procedure to follow ordinarily is to   3._____

    A. informally chat with the applicant in your office until your supervisor has finished his phone conversation
    B. escort him directly into your supervisor's office and have him wait for him there
    C. inform your supervisor of the applicant's arrival and try to make the applicant feel comfortable while waiting
    D. have him hang up his coat and tell him to go directly in to see your supervisor

Questions 4-9.

DIRECTIONS: Questions 4 through 9 each consist of a sentence which may or may not be an example of good English usage. Consider grammar, punctuation, spelling, capitalization, awkwardness, etc. Examine each sentence, and then choose the correct statement about it from the four choices below it. If the English usage in the sentence given is better than any of the changes suggested in options B, C, or D, choose option A. Do not choose an option that will change the meaning of the sentence.

4. The report, along with the accompanying documents, were submitted for review.   4._____

    A. This is an example of acceptable writing.
    B. The words *were submitted* should be changed to *was submitted*.
    C. The word *accompanying* should be spelled *accompaning*.
    D. The comma after the word *report* should be taken out.

5. If others must use your files, be certain that they understand how the system works, but insist that you do all the filing and refiling.

    A. This is an example of acceptable writing.
    B. There should be a period after the word *works*, and the word *but* should start a new sentence.
    C. The words *filing* and *refiling* should be spelled *fileing* and *refileing*.
    D. There should be a comma after the word *but*.

6. The appeal was not considered because of its late arrival.

    A. This is an example of acceptable writing.
    B. The word *its* should be changed to *it's*.
    C. The word *its* should be changed to *the*.
    D. The words *late arrival* should be changed to *arrival late*.

7. The letter must be read carefuly to determine under which subject it should be filed.

    A. This is an example of acceptable writing.
    B. The word *under* should be changed to *at*.
    C. The word *determine* should be spelled *determin*.
    D. The word *carefuly* should be spelled *carefully*.

8. He showed potential as an office manager, but he lacked skill in delegating work.

    A. This is an example of acceptable writing.
    B. The word *delegating* should be spelled *delagating*.
    C. The word *potential* should be spelled *potencial*.
    D. The words *lie lacked* should be changed to *was lacking*.

9. His supervisor told him that it would be all right to receive personal mail at the office.

    A. This is an example of acceptable writing.
    B. The words *all right* should be changed to *alright*.
    C. The word *personal* should be spelled *personel*.
    D. The word *mail* should be changed to *letters*.

Questions 10-13.

DIRECTIONS: Questions 10 through 13 are to be answered SOLELY on the basis of the information given in the following passage.

Typed pages can reflect the simplicity of modern art in a machine age. Lightness and evenness can be achieved by proper layout and balance of typed lines and white space. Instead of solid, cramped masses of uneven, crowded typing, there should be a pleasing balance up and down as well as horizontal.

To have real balance, your page must have a center. The eyes see the center of the sheet slightly above the real center. This is the way both you and the reader see it. Try imagining a line down the center of the page that divides the paper in equal halves. On either side of your paper, white space and blocks of typing need to be similar in size and shape. Although left and right margins should be equal, top and bottom margins need not be as exact. It looks better to hold a bottom border wider than a top margin, so that your typing rests *upon a cushion of white space. To add interest to the appearance of the page, try making one paragraph between one-half and two-thirds the size of an adjacent paragraph.*

Thus, by taking full advantage of your typewriter, the pages that you type will not only be accurate but will also be attractive.

10. It can be inferred from the passage that the BASIC importance of proper balancing on a typed page is that proper balancing

    10.____

    A. makes a typed page a work of modern art
    B. provides exercise in proper positioning of a typewriter
    C. increases the amount of typed copy on the paper
    D. draws greater attention and interest to the page

11. A reader will tend to see the center of a typed page

    11.____

    A. somewhat higher than the true center
    B. somewhat lower than the true center
    C. on either side of the true center
    D. about two-thirds of an inch above the true center

12. Which of the following suggestions is NOT given by the passage?

    12.____

    A. Bottom margins may be wider than top borders.
    B. Keep all paragraphs approximately the same size.
    C. Divide your page with an imaginary line down the middle.
    D. Side margins should be equalized.

13. Of the following, the BEST title for this passage is:

    13.____

    A. INCREASING THE ACCURACY OF THE TYPED PAGE
    B. DETERMINATION OF MARGINS FOR TYPED COPY
    C. LAYOUT AND BALANCE OF THE TYPED PAGE
    D. HOW TO TAKE FULL ADVANTAGE OF THE TYPEWRITER

14. In order to type addresses on a large number of envelopes MOST efficiently, you should

    14.____

    A. insert another envelope into the typewriter before removing each typed envelope
    B. take each typed envelope out of the machine before starting the next envelope
    C. insert several envelopes into the machine at one time, keeping all top and bottom edges even
    D. insert several envelopes into the machine at one time, keeping the top edge of each envelope two inches below the top edge of the one beneath it

15. A senior typist has completed copying a statistical report from a rough draft.
Of the following, the BEST way to be sure that her typing is correct is for the typist to

    15.____

    A. fold the rough draft, line it up with the typed copy, compare one-half of the columns with the original, and have a co-worker compare the other half
    B. check each line of the report as it is typed and then have a co-worker check each line again after the entire report is finished

C. have a co-worker add each column and check the totals on the typed copy with the totals on the original

D. have a co-worker read aloud from the rough draft while the typist checks the typed copy and then have the typist read while the co-worker checks

16. In order to center a heading when typing a report, you should   16.____

    A. measure your typing paper with a ruler and begin the heading one-third of the way in from the left margin

    B. begin the heading at the point on the typewriter scale which is 50 minus the number of letters in the heading

    C. multiply the number of characters in the heading by two and begin the heading that number of spaces in from the left margin

    D. begin the heading at the point on the scale which is equal to the center point of your paper minus one-half the number of characters and spaces in the heading

17. Which of the following recommendations concerning the use of copy paper for making typewritten copies should NOT be followed?   17.____

    A. Copy papers should be checked for wrinkles before being used.

    B. Legal-size copy paper may be folded if it is too large to fit into a convenient drawer space.

    C. When several sheets of paper are being used, they should be fastened with a paper clip at the top after insertion in the typewriter.

    D. For making many copies, paper of the same weight and brightness should be used.

18. Assume that a new typist, Norma Garcia, has been assigned to work under your supervision and is reporting to work for the first time. You formally introduce Norma to her co-workers and suggest that a few of the other typists explain the office procedures and typing formats to her. The practice of instructing Norma in her duties in this manner is   18.____

    A. *good* because she will be made to feel at home

    B. *good* because she will learn more about routine office tasks from co-workers than from you

    C. *poor* because her co-workers will resent the extra work

    D. *poor* because you will not have enough control over her training

19. Suppose that Jean Brown, a typist, is typing a letter following the same format that she has always used. However, she notices that the other two typists in her office are also typing letters, but are using a different format. Jean is concerned that she might not have been informed of a change in format.   19.____
Of the following, the FIRST action that Jean should take is to

    A. seek advice from her supervisor as to which format to use

    B. ask the other typists whether she should use a new format for typing letters

    C. disregard the format that the other typists are using and continue to type in the format she had been using

    D. use the format that the other typists are using, assuming that it is a newly accepted method

20. Suppose that the new office to which you have been assigned has put up Christmas dec-   20.____
    orations, and a Christmas party is being planned by the city agency in which you work.
    However, nothing has been said about Christmas gifts.
    It would be CORRECT for you to assume that

    A.   you are expected to give a gift to your supervisor
    B.   your supervisor will give you a gift
    C.   you are expected to give gifts only to your subordinates
    D.   you will neither receive gifts nor will you be expected to give any

---

KEY (CORRECT ANSWERS)

1.	B		11.	A
2.	D		12.	B
3.	C		13.	C
4.	B		14.	A
5.	A		15.	D
6.	A		16.	D
7.	D		17.	B
8.	A		18.	D
9.	A		19.	A
10.	D		20.	D

TEST 2

DIRECTIONS: Each question or incomplete statement is followed by several suggested answers or completions. Select the one that BEST answers the question or completes the statement. *PRINT THE LETTER OF THE CORRECT ANSWER IN THE SPACE AT THE RIGHT.*

1. The supervisor you assist is under great pressure to meet certain target dates. He has scheduled an emergency meeting to take place in a few days, and he asks you to send out notices immediately. As you begin to prepare the notices, however, you realize he has scheduled the meeting for a Saturday, which is not a working day. Also, you sense that your supervisor is not in a good mood.
   Which of the following is the MOST effective method of handling this situation?

   A. Change the meeting date to the first working day after that Saturday and send out the notices.
   B. Change the meeting date to a working day on which his calendar is clear and send out the notices.
   C. Point out to your supervisor that the date is a Saturday.
   D. Send out the notices as they are since you have received specific instructions.

1.____

Questions 2-7.

DIRECTIONS: Questions 2 through 7 each consist of a sentence which may or may not be an example of good English usage. Consider grammar, punctuation, spelling, capitalization, awkwardness, etc. Examine each sentence, and then choose the correct statement about it from the four choices below it. If the English usage in the sentence given is better than any of the changes suggested in options B, C, or D, choose option A. Do not choose an option that will change the meaning of the sentence.

2. The typist used an extention cord in order to connect her typewriter to the outlet nearest to her desk.

   A. This is an example of acceptable writing.
   B. A period should be placed after the word *cord,* and the word *in* should have a capital I.
   C. A comma should be placed after the word *typewriter.*
   D. The word *extention* should be spelled *extension.*

2.____

3. He would have went to the conference if he had received an invitation.

   A. This is an example of acceptable writing.
   B. The word *went* should be replaced by the word *gone.*
   C. The word *had* should be replaced by *would have.*
   D. The word *conference* should be spelled *conferance.*

3.____

4. In order to make the report neater, he spent many hours rewriting it.

   A. This is an example of acceptable writing.
   B. The word *more* should be inserted before the word *neater.*
   C. There should be a colon after the word *neater.*
   D. The word *spent* should be changed to *have spent.*

4.____

5. His supervisor told him that he should of read the memorandum more carefully.   5.____

    A. This is an example of acceptable writing.
    B. The word *memorandum* should be spelled *memorandom*.
    C. The word *of* should be replaced by the word *have*.
    D. The word *carefully* should be replaced by the word *careful*.

6. It was decided that two separate reports should be written.   6.____

    A. This is an example of acceptable writing.
    B. A comma should be inserted after the word *decided*.
    C. The word *be* should be replaced by the word *been*.
    D. A colon should be inserted after the word *that*.

7. She don't seem to understand that the work must be done as soon as possible.   7.____

    A. This is an example of acceptable writing.
    B. The word *doesn't* should replace the word *don't*.
    C. The word *why* should replace the word *that*.
    D. The word *as* before the word *soon* should be eliminated.

Questions 8-11.

DIRECTIONS: Questions 8 through 11 are to be answered SOLELY on the basis of the following passage.

There is nothing that will take the place of good sense on the part of the stenographer. You may be perfect in transcribing exactly what the dictator says and your speed may be adequate; but without an understanding of the dictator's intent as well as his words, you are likely to be a mediocre secretary.

A serious error that is made when taking dictation is putting down something that does not make sense. Most people who dictate material would rather be asked to repeat and explain than to receive transcribed material which has errors due to inattention or doubt. Many dictators request that their grammar be corrected by their secretaries; but unless specifically asked to do so, secretaries should not do it without first checking with the dictator. Secretaries should be aware that, in some cases, dictators may use incorrect grammar or slang expressions to create a particular effect.

Some people dictate commas, periods, and paragraphs, while others expect the stenographer to know when, where, and how to punctuate. A well-trained secretary should be able to indicate the proper punctuation by listening to the pauses and tones of the dictator's voice.

A stenographer who has taken dictation from the same person for a period of time should be able to understand him under most conditions. By increasing her tact, alertness, and efficiency, a secretary can become more competent.

8. According to the passage, which of the following statements concerning the dictation of   8.____
punctuation is CORRECT?
A

    A. dictator may use incorrect punctuation to create a desired style

B. dictator should indicate all punctuation

C. stenographer should know how to punctuate based on the pauses and tones of the dictator

D. stenographer should not type any punctuation if it has not been dictated to her

9. According to the passage, how should secretaries handle grammatical errors in a dictation?
Secretaries should

A. *not correct* grammatical errors unless the dictator is aware that this is being done

B. *correct* grammatical errors by having the dictator repeat the line with proper pauses

C. *correct* grammatical errors if they have checked the correctness in a grammar book

D. *correct* grammatical errors based on their own good sense

9.___

10. If a stenographer is confused about the method of spacing and indenting of a report which has just been dictated to her, she GENERALLY should

A. do the best she can

B. ask the dictator to explain what she should do

C. try to improve her ability to understand dictated material

D. accept the fact that her stenographic ability is not adequate

10.___

11. In the last line of the first paragraph, the word *mediocre* means MOST NEARLY

A. superior
C. respected
B. disregarded
D. second-rate

11.___

12. Assume that is is your responsibility to schedule meetings for your supervisor, who believes in starting these meetings strictly on time. He has told you to schedule separate meetings with Mr. Smith and Ms. Jones, which will last approximately 20 minutes each. You have told Mr. Smith to arrive at 10:00 A.M. and Ms. Jones at 10:30 A.M. Your supervisor will have an hour of free time at 11:00 A.M. At 10:25 A.M., Mr. Smith arrives and states that there was a train delay, and he is sorry that he is late. Ms. Jones has not yet arrived. You do not know who Mr. Smith and Ms. Jones are or what the meetings will be about.
Of the following, the BEST course of action for you to take is to

A. send Mr. Smith in to see your supervisor; and when Ms. Jones arrives, tell her that your supervisor's first meeting will take more time than he expected

B. tell Mr. Smith that your supervisor has a meeting at 10:30 A.M. and that you will have to reschedule his meeting for another day

C. check with your supervisor to find out if he would prefer to see Mr. Smith immediately or at 11:00 A.M.

D. encourage your supervisor to meet with Mr. Smith immediately because Mr. Smith's late arrival was not intentional

12.___

13. Assume that you have been told by your boss not to let anyone disturb him for the rest of the afternoon unless absolutely necessary since he has to complete some urgent work. His supervisor, who is the bureau chief, telephones and asks to speak to him.
The BEST course of action for you to take is to

13.___

A.   ask the bureau chief if he can leave a message
B.   ask your boss if he can take the call
C.   tell the bureau chief that your boss is out
D.   tell your boss that his instructions will get you into trouble

14.   Which one of the following is the MOST advisable procedure for a stenographer to follow   14._____
when a dictator asks her to make extra copies of dictated material?

A.   Note the number of copies required at the beginning of the notes.
B.   Note the number of copies required at the end of the notes.
C.   Make a mental note of the number of copies required to be made.
D.   Make a checkmark beside the notes to serve as a reminder that extra copies are required.

15.   Suppose that, as you are taking shorthand notes, the dictator tells you that the sentence   15._____
he has just dictated is to be deleted.
Of the following, the BEST thing for you to do is to

A.   place the correction in the left-hand margin next to the deleted sentence
B.   write the word *delete* over the sentence and place the correction on a separate page for corrections
C.   erase the sentence and use that available space for the correction
D.   draw a line through the sentence and begin the correction on the next available line

16.   Assume that your supervisor, who normally dictates at a relatively slow rate, begins dic-   16._____
tating to you very rapidly. You find it very difficult to keep up at this speed. Which one of
the following is the BEST action to take in this situation?

A.   Ask your supervisor to dictate more slowly since you are having difficulty.
B.   Continue to take the dictation at the fast speed and fill in the blanks later.
C.   Interrupt your supervisor with a question about the dictation, hoping that when she begins again it will be slower.
D.   Refuse to take the dictation unless given at the speed indicated in your job description.

17.   Assume that you have been asked to put a heading on the second, third, and fourth   17._____
pages of a four-page letter to make sure they can be identified in case they are separated from the first page.
Which of the following is it LEAST important to include in such a heading?

A.   Date of the letter
B.   Initials of the typist
C.   Name of the person to whom the letter is addressed
D.   Number of the page

18.   Which one of the following is NOT generally accepted when dividing words at the end of   18._____
a line?
Dividing

A.   a hyphenated word at the hyphen
B.   a word immediately after the prefix
C.   a word immediately before the suffix
D.   proper names between syllables

19. In the preparation of a business letter which has two enclosures, the MOST generally   19.____
accepted of the following procedures to follow is to type

    A. *See Attached Items* one line below the last line of the body of the letter
    B. *See Attached Enclosures* to the left of the signature
    C. *Enclosures 2* at the left margin below the signature line
    D. nothing on the letter to indicate enclosures since it will be obvious to the reader
    that there are enclosures in the envelope

20. Standard rules for typing spacing have developed through usage.   20.____
According to these rules, one space is left AFTER

    A. a comma   B. every sentence
    C. a colon   D. an opening parenthesis

KEY (CORRECT ANSWERS)

1.	C		11.	D
2.	D		12.	C
3.	B		13.	B
4.	A		14.	A
5.	C		15.	D
6.	A		16.	A
7.	B		17.	B
8.	C		18.	D
9.	A		19.	C
10.	B		20.	A

EXAMINATION SECTION
TEST 1

Questions 1-10.

WORD MEANING

1. ACCURATE   1.____
 A. correct B. useful C. afraid D. careless

2. ALTER   2.____
 A. copy B. change C. report D. agree

3. DOCUMENT   3.____
 A. outline B. agreement C. blueprint D. record

4. INDICATE   4.____
 A. listen B. show C. guess D. try

5. INVENTORY   5.____
 A. custom B. discovery C. warning D. list

6. ISSUE   6.____
 A. annoy B. use up C. give out D. gain

7. NOTIFY   7.____
 A. inform B. promise C. approve D. strengthen

8. ROUTINE   8.____
 A. path B. mistake C. habit D. journey

9. TERMINATE   9.____
 A. rest B. start C. deny D. end

10. TRANSMIT   10.____
 A. put in B. send C. stop D. go across

Questions 11-15.

READING COMPREHENSION

DIRECTIONS: Questions 11 through 15 test how well you understand what you read. It will be necessary for you to read carefully because your answers to these questions should be based ONLY on the information given in the following paragraphs.

The recipient gains an impression of a typewritten letter before he begins to read the message. Pastors which provide for a good first impression include margins and spacing that are visually pleasing, formal parts of the letter which are correctly placed according to the style of the letter, copy which is free of obvious erasures and over-strikes, and transcript that is even and clear. The problem for the typist is that of how to produce that first, positive impression of her work.

There are several general rules which a typist can follow when she wishes to prepare a properly spaced letter on a sheet of letter-head. Ordinarily, the width of a letter should not be less than four inches nor more than six inches. The side margins should also have a desirable relation to the bottom margin and the space between the letterhead and the body of the letter. Usually the most appealing arrangement is when the side margins are even and the bottom margin is slightly wider than the side margins. In some offices, however, standard line length is used for all business letters, and the secretary then varies the spacing between the date line and the inside address according to the length of the letter.

11. The BEST title for the above paragraphs would be:

    A. Writing Office Letters
    B. Making Good First Impressions
    C. Judging Well-Typed Letters
    D. Good Placing and Spacing for Office Letters

11.____

12. According to the above paragraphs, which of the following might be considered the way in which people very quickly judge the quality of work which has been typed? By

    A. measuring the margins to see if they are correct
    B. looking at the spacing and cleanliness of the typescript
    C. scanning the body of the letter for meaning
    D. reading the date line and address for errors

12.____

13. What, according to the above paragraphs, would be definitely UNDESIRABLE as the average line length of a typed letter?

    A. 4"   B. 5"   C. 6"   D. 7"

13.____

14. According to the above paragraphs, when the line length is kept standard, the secretary

    A. does not have to vary the spacing at all since this also is standard
    B. adjusts the spacing between the date line and inside address for different lengths of letters
    C. uses the longest line as a guideline for spacing between the date line and inside address
    D. varies the number of spaces between the lines

14.____

15. According to the above paragraphs, side margins are MOST pleasing when they   15.____

    A. are even and somewhat smaller than the bottom margin
    B. are slightly wider than the bottom margin
    C. vary with the length of the letter
    D. are figured independently from the letterhead and the body of the letter

Questions 16-20.

CODING

DIRECTIONS:

Name of Applicant	H A N G S B R U K E
Test Code	c o m p l e x i t y
File Number	0 1 2 3 4 5 6 7 8 9

Assume that each of the above capital letters is the first letter of the name of an Applicant, that the small letter directly beneath each capital letter is the test code for the Applicant, and that the number directly beneath each code letter is the file number for the Applicant.

In each of the following Questions 16 through 20, the test code letters and the file numbers in Columns 2 and 3 should correspond to the capital letters in Column 1. For each question, look at each column carefully and mark your answer as follows:

    If there is an error only in Column 2, mark your
    answer A.
    If there is an error only in Column 3, mark your
    answer B.
    If there is an error in both Columns 2 and 3, mark
    your answer C.
    If both Columns 2 and 3 are correct, mark your
    answer D.

The following sample question is given to help you understand the procedure.

SAMPLE QUESTION

Column 1	Column 2	Column 3
AKEHN	otyci	18902

In Column 2, the final test code letter *i.* should be *m.* Column 3 is correctly coded to Column 1. Since there is an error only in Column 2, the answer is A.

	Column 1	Column 2	Column 3	
16.	NEKKU	mytti	29987	16.____
17.	KRAEB	txyle	86095	17.____
18.	ENAUK	ymoit	92178	18.____
19.	REANA	xeomo	69121	19.____
20.	EKHSE	ytcxy	97049	20.____

Questions 21-30.

ARITHMETICAL REASONING

21. If a secretary answered 28 phone calls and typed the addresses for 112 credit statements in one morning, what is the ratio of phone calls answered to credit statements typed for that period of time?

    A. 1:4   B. 1:7   C. 2:3   D. 3:5

21.____

22. According to a suggested filing system, no more than 10 folders should be filed behind any one file guide and from 15 to 25 file guides should be used in each file drawer for easy finding and filing.
The maximum number of folders that a five-drawer file cabinet can hold to allow easy finding and filing is

    A. 550   B. 750   C. 1,100   D. 1,250

22.____

23. An employee had a starting salary of $25,804. He received a salary increase at the end of each year, and at the end of the seventh year his salary was $33,476.
What was his average annual increase in salary over these seven years?

    A. $1,020   B. $1,076   C. $1,096   D. $1,144

23.____

24. The 55 typists and 28 senior clerks in a certain city agency were paid a total of $1,943,200 in salaries last year.
If the average annual salary of a typist was $22,400 the average annual salary of a senior clerk was

    A. $25,400   B. $26,600   C. $26,800   D. $27,000

24.____

25. A typist has been given a three page report to type. She has finished typing the first two pages. The first page has 283 words, and the second page has 366 words.
If the total report consists of 954 words, how many words will she have to type on the third page of the report?

    A. 202   B. 287   C. 305   D. 313

25.____

26. In one day, Clerk A processed 30% more forms than Clerk B, and Clerk C processed li times as many forms as Clerk A. If Clerk B processed 40 forms, how many more forms were processed by Clerk C than Clerk B?

    A. 12   B. 13   C. 21   D. 25

26.____

27. A clerk who earns a gross salary of $452 every two weeks has the following deductions taken from her paycheck:
15% for City, State, Federal taxes; 2 1/2% for Social Security; $1.30 for health insurance; and $6.00 for union dues. The amount of her take-home pay is

    A. $256.20   B. $312.40   C. $331.60   D. $365.60

27.____

28. In 2005, a city agency spent $2,000 to buy pencils at a cost of $5.00 a dozen.
If the agency used 3/4 of these pencils in 2005 and used the same number of pencils in 2006, how many more pencils did it have to buy to have enough pencils for all of 2006?

    A. 1,200   B. 2,400   C. 3,600   D. 4,800

28.____

29. A clerk who worked in Agency X earned the following salaries: $20,140 the first year,$21,000 the second year, and $21,920 the third year. Another clerk who worked in Agency Y for three years earned $21,100 a year for two years and $21,448 the third year. The difference between the average salaries received by both clerks over a three-year period is   29.____

    A. $196   B. $204   C. $348   D. $564

30. An employee who works over 40 hours in any week receives overtime payment for the extra hours at time and one-half (1 1/2 times) his hourly rate of pay. An employee who earns $13.60 an hour works a total of 45 hours during a certain week.
His total pay for that week would be   30.____

    A. $564.40   B. $612.00   C. $646.00   D. $812.00

Questions 31-35.

RELATED INFORMATION

31. To tell a newly-employed clerk to fill a top drawer of a four-drawer cabinet with heavy folders which will be often used and to keep lower drawers only partly filled is   31.____

    A. *good,* because a tall person would have to bend unnecessarily if he had to use a lower drawer
    B. *bad,* because the file cabinet may tip over when the top drawer is opened
    C. *good,* because it is the most easily reachable drawer for the average person
    D. *bad,* because a person bending down at another drawer may accidentally bang his head on the bottom of the drawer when he straightens up

32. If a senior typist or senior clerk has requisitioned a *ream* of paper in order to duplicate a single page office announcement, how many announcements can be printed from the one package of paper?   32.____

    A. 200   B. 500   C. 700   D. 1,000

33. Your supervisor has asked you to locate a telephone number for an attorney named Jones, whose office is located at 311 Broadway, and whose name is not already listed in your files.
The BEST method for finding the number would be for you to   33.____

    A. call the information operator and have her get it for you
    B. look in the alphabetical directory (white pages) under the name Jones at 311 Broadway
    C. refer to the heading Attorney in the yellow pages for the name Jones at 311 Broadway
    D. ask your supervisor who referred her to Mr. Jones, then call that person for the number

34. An example of material that should NOT be sent by first class mail is a   34.____

    A. email copy of a letter   B. post card
    C. business reply card   D. large catalogue

35. In the operations of a government agency, a voucher is ORDINARILY used to   35._____

    A. refer someone to the agency for a position or assignment
    B. certify that an agency's records of financial trans-actions are accurate
    C. order payment from agency funds of a stated amount to an individual
    D. enter a statement of official opinion in the records of the agency

Questions 36-40.

ENGLISH USAGE

DIRECTIONS: Each question from 36 through 40 contains a sentence. Read each sentence carefully to decide whether it is correct. Then, in the space at the right, mark your answer:

    (A) if the sentence is incorrect because of bad grammar or sentence structure

    (B) if the sentence is incorrect because of bad punctuation

    (C) if the sentence is incorrect because of bad capitalization

    (D) if the sentence is correct

    Each incorrect sentence has only one type of error. Consider a sentence correct if it has no errors, although there may be other correct ways of saying the same thing.

    SAMPLE QUESTION I: One of our clerks were promoted yesterday.

    The subject of this sentence is *one,* so the verb should be *was promoted* instead of *were promoted.* Since the sentence is incorrect because of bad grammar, the answer to Sample Question I is (A).

    SAMPLE QUESTION II: Between you and me, I would prefer not going there.

    Since this sentence is correct, the answer to Sample Question II is (D).

36. The National alliance of Businessmen is trying to persuade private businesses to hire   36._____
youth in the summertime.

37. The supervisor who is on vacation, is in charge of processing vouchers.   37._____

38. The activity of the committee at its conferences is always stimulating.   38._____

39. After checking the addresses again, the letters went to the mailroom.   39._____

40. The director, as well as the employees, are interested in sharing the dividends.   40._____

Questions 41-45.

FILING

DIRECTIONS: Each question from 41 through 45 contains four names. For each question, choose the name that should be FIRST if the four names are to be arranged in alphabeti-cal order in accordance with the Rules for Alphabetical Filing given below. Read these rules carefully. Then, for each question, indicate in the space at the right the letter before the name that should be FIRST in alphabet-ical order.

RULES FOR ALPHABETICAL FILING

Names of People

(1)   The names of people are filed in strict alphabetical order, first according to the last name, then according to first name or initial, and finally according to middle name or initial. FOR EXAMPLE: George Allen comes before Edward Bell, and Leonard P. Reston comes before Lucille B. Reston.

(2)   When last names are the same, FOR EXAMPLE, A. Green and Agnes Green, the one with the initial comes before the one with the name written out when the first initials are identi-cal.

(3)   When first and last names are alike and the middle name is given, FOR EXAMPLE, John David Doe and John Devoe Doe, the names should be filed in the alphabetical order of the middle names.

(4)   When first and last names are the same, a name without a middle initial comes before one with a middle name or initial. FOR EXAMPLE, John Doe comes before both John A. Doe and John Alan Doe.

(5)   When first and last names are the same, a name with a middle initial comes before one with a middle name beginning with the same initial. FOR EXAMPLE: Jack R. Hertz comes before Jack Richard Hertz.

(6)   Prefixes such as De, O', Mac, Mc, and Van are filed as written and are treated as part of the names to which they are connected. FOR EXAMPLE: Robert O'Dea is filed before David Olsen.

(7)   Abbreviated names are treated as if they were spelled out. FOR EXAMPLE: Chas. is filed as Charles and Thos. is filed as Thomas.

(8)   Titles and designations such as Dr., Mr., and Prof, are disregarded in filing.

Names of Organizations

(1)   The names of business organizations are filed according to the order in which each word in the name appears. When an organization name bears the name of a person, it is filed according to the rules for filing names of people as given above. FOR EXAMPLE: William Smith Service Co. comes before Television Distributors, Inc.

(2) *Where bureau, board, office, or department appears as the first part of the title of a governmental agency, that agency should be filed under the word in the title expressing the chief function of the agency. FOR EXAMPLE: Bureau of the Budget would be filed as if written Budget, (Bureau of the). The Department of Personnel would be filed as if written Personnel, (Department of).*

(3) *When the following words are part of an organization, they are disregarded: the, of, and.*

(4) *When there are numbers in a name, they are treated as if they were spelled out. FOR EXAMPLE: 10th Street Bootery is filed as Tenth Street Bootery.*

SAMPLE QUESTION:

A.	Jane Earl	(2)
B.	James A. Earle	(4)
C.	James Earl	(1)
D.	J. Earle	(3)

The numbers in parentheses show the proper alphabetical order in which these names should be filed. Since the name that should be filed FIRST is James Earl, the answer to the Sample Question is (C).

41.
A. Majorca Leather Goods
B. Robert Maiorca and Sons
C. Maintenance Management Corp.
D. Majestic Carpet Mills
    41._____

42.
A. Municipal Telephone Service
B. Municipal Reference Library
C. Municipal Credit Union
D. Municipal Broadcasting System
    42._____

43.
A. Robert B. Pierce   B. R. Bruce Pierce
C. Ronald Pierce   D. Robert Bruce Pierce
    43._____

44.
A. Four Seasons Sports Club   B. 14th. St. Shopping Center
C. Forty Thieves Restaurant   D. 42nd St. Theaters
    44._____

45.
A. Franco Franceschini   B. Amos Franchini
C. Sandra Franceschia   D. Lilie Franchinesca
    45._____

Questions 46-50.

SPELLING

DIRECTIONS: In each question, one of the words is misspelled. Select the letter of the misspelled word. *PRINT THE LETTER OF THE CORRECT ANSWER IN THE SPACE AT THE RIGHT.*

46.
A. option   B. extradite
C. comparitive   D. jealousy
    46._____

47.
A. handicaped   B. assurance
C. sympathy   D. speech
    47._____

48.	A. recommend	B. carraige		48.____
	C. disapprove	D. independent		
49.	A. ingenuity	B. tenet (opinion)		49.____
	C. uncanny	D. intrigueing		
50.	A. arduous	B. hideous		50.____
	C. iervant	D. companies		

KEY (CORRECT ANSWERS)

1. A	11. D	21. A	31. B	41. C
2. B	12. B	22. D	32. B	42. D
3. D	13. D	23. C	33. C	43. B
4. B	14. B	24. A	34. D	44. D
5. D	15. A	25. C	35. C	45. C
6. C	16. B	26. D	36. C	46. C
7. A	17. C	27. D	37. B	47. A
8. C	18. D	28. B	38. D	48. B
9. D	19. A	29. A	39. A	49. D
10. B	20. C	30. C	40. A	50. C'

RECORD KEEPING
EXAMINATION SECTION
TEST 1

DIRECTIONS: Each question or incomplete statement is followed by several suggested answers or completions. Select the one that BEST answers the question or completes the statement. *PRINT THE LETTER OF THE CORRECT ANSWER IN THE SPACE AT THE RIGHT.*

Questions 1-15.

DIRECTIONS: Questions 1 through 15 are to be answered on the basis of the following list of company names below. Arrange a file alphabetically, word-by-word, disregarding punctuation, conjunctions, and apostrophes. Then answer the questions.

A Bee C Reading Materials
ABCO Parts
A Better Course for Test Preparation
AAA Auto Parts Co.
A-Z Auto Parts, Inc.
Aabar Books
Abbey, Joanne
Boman-Sylvan Law Firm
BMW Autowerks
C Q Service Company
Chappell-Murray, Inc.
E&E Life Insurance
Emcrisco
Gigi Arts
Gordon, Jon & Associates
SOS Plumbing
Schmidt, J.B. Co.

1. Which of these files should appear FIRST?   1.____

    A. ABCO Parts
    B. A Bee C Reading Materials
    C. A Better Course for Test Preparation
    D. AAA Auto Parts Co.

2. Which of these files should appear SECOND?   2.____

    A. A-Z Auto Parts, Inc.
    B. A Bee C Reading Materials
    C. A Better Course for Test Preparation
    D. AAA Auto Parts Co.

3. Which of these files should appear THIRD?   3.____

    A. ABCO Parts
    B. A Bee C Reading Materials
    C. Aabar Books
    D. AAA Auto Parts Co.

4. Which of these files should appear FOURTH? 4.___

    A. Aabar Books
    B. ABCO Parts
    C. Abbey, Joanne
    D. AAA Auto Parts Co.

5. Which of these files should appear LAST? 5.___

    A. Gordon, Jon & Associates
    B. Gigi Arts
    C. Schmidt, J.B. Co.
    D. SOS Plumbing

6. Which of these files should appear between A-Z Auto Parts, Inc. and Abbey, Joanne? 6.___

    A. A Bee C Reading Materials
    B. AAA Auto Parts Co.
    C. ABCO Parts
    D. A Better Course for Test Preparation

7. Which of these files should appear between ABCO Parts and Aabar Books? 7.___

    A. A Bee C Reading Materials
    B. Abbey, Joanne
    C. Aabar Books
    D. A-Z Auto Parts

8. Which of these files should appear between Abbey, Joanne and Boman-Sylvan Law Firm? 8.___

    A. A Better Course for Test Preparation
    B. BMW Autowerks
    C. Chappell-Murray, Inc.
    D. Aabar Books

9. Which of these files should appear between Abbey, Joanne and C Q Service? 9.___

    A. A-Z Auto Parts,Inc.   B. BMW Autowerks
    C. Choices A and B   D. Chappell-Murray, Inc.

10. Which of these files should appear between C Q Service Company and Emcrisco? 10.___

    A. Chappell-Murray, Inc.   B. E&E Life Insurance
    C. Gigi Arts   D. Choices A and B

11. Which of these files should NOT appear between C Q Service Company and E&E Life Insurance? 11.___

    A. Gordon, Jon & Associates
    B. Emcrisco
    C. Gigi Arts
    D. All of the above

12. Which of these files should appear between Chappell-Murray Inc., and Gigi Arts?   12.____

    A. CQ Service Inc. E&E Life Insurance, and Emcrisco
    B. Emcrisco, E&E Life Insurance, and Gordon, Jon & Associates
    C. E&E Life Insurance and Emcrisco
    D. Emcrisco and Gordon, Jon & Associates

13. Which of these files should appear between Gordon, Jon & Associates and SOS Plumb-   13.____
ing?

    A. Gigi Arts   B. Schmidt, J.B. Co.
    C. Choices A and B   D. None of the above

14. Each of the choices lists the four files in their proper alphabetical order except   14.____

    A. E&E Life Insurance; Gigi Arts; Gordon, Jon & Associates; SOS Plumbing
    B. E&E Life Insurance; Emcrisco; Gigi Arts; SOS Plumbing
    C. Emcrisco; Gordon, Jon & Associates; SOS Plumbing; Schmidt, J.B. Co.
    D. Emcrisco; Gigi Arts; Gordon, Jon & Associates; SOS Plumbing

15. Which of the choices lists the four files in their proper alphabetical order?   15.____

    A. Gigi Arts; Gordon, Jon & Associates; SOS Plumbing; Schmidt, J.B. Co.
    B. Gordon, Jon & Associates; Gigi Arts; Schmidt, J.B. Co.; SOS Plumbing
    C. Gordon, Jon & Associates; Gigi Arts; SOS Plumbing; Schmidt, J.B. Co.
    D. Gigi Arts; Gordon, Jon & Associates; Schmidt, J.B. Co.; SOS Plumbing

16. The alphabetical filing order of two businesses with identical names is determined by the   16.____

    A. length of time each business has been operating
    B. addresses of the businesses
    C. last name of the company president
    D. none of the above

17. In an alphabetical filing system, if a business name includes a number, it should be   17.____

    A. disregarded
    B. considered a number and placed at the end of an alphabetical section
    C. treated as though it were written in words and alphabetized accordingly
    D. considered a number and placed at the beginning of an alphabetical section

18. If a business name includes a contraction (such as *don't* or *it's*), how should that word be   18.____
treated in an alphabetical filing system?

    A. Divide the word into its separate parts and treat it as two words.
    B. Ignore the letters that come after the apostrophe.
    C. Ignore the word that contains the contraction.
    D. Ignore the apostrophe and consider all letters in the contraction.

19. In what order should the parts of an address be considered when using an alphabetical   19.____
filing system?

    A. City or town; state; street name; house or building number
    B. State; city or town; street name; house or building number
    C. House or building number; street name; city or town; state
    D. Street name; city or town; state

20. A business record should be cross-referenced when a(n)   20.___

    A. organization is known by an abbreviated name
    B. business has a name change because of a sale, incorporation, or other reason
    C. business is known by a *coined* or common name which differs from a dictionary spelling
    D. all of the above

21. A geographical filing system is MOST effective when   21.___

    A. location is more important than name
    B. many names or titles sound alike
    C. dealing with companies who have offices all over the world
    D. filing personal and business files

Questions 22-25.

DIRECTIONS: Questions 22 through 25 are to be answered on the basis of the list of items below, which are to be filed geographically. Organize the items geographically and then answer the questions.
    1. University Press at Berkeley, U.S.
    2. Maria Sanchez, Mexico City, Mexico
    3. Great Expectations Ltd. in London, England
    4. Justice League, Cape Town, South Africa, Africa
    5. Crown Pearls Ltd. in London, England
    6. Joseph Prasad in London, England

22. Which of the following arrangements of the items is composed according to the policy of: 22.___
Continent, Country, City, Firm or Individual Name?

    A. 5, 3, 4, 6, 2, 1   B. 4, 5, 3, 6, 2, 1
    C. 1, 4, 5, 3, 6, 2   D. 4, 5, 3, 6, 1, 2

23. Which of the following files is arranged according to the policy of: *Continent, Country,*   23.___
City, Firm or Individual Name?

    A. South Africa. Africa. Cape Town. Justice League
    B. Mexico. Mexico City, Maria Sanchez
    C. North America. United States. Berkeley. University Press
    D. England. Europe. London. Prasad, Joseph

24. Which of the following arrangements of the items is composed according to the policy of: 24.___
Country, City, Firm or Individual Name?

    A. 5, 6, 3, 2, 4, 1   B. 1, 5, 6, 3, 2, 4
    C. 6, 5, 3, 2, 4, 1   D. 5, 3, 6, 2, 4, 1

25. Which of the following files is arranged according to a policy of: *Country, City, Firm or*   25.___
Individual Name?

    A. England. London. Crown Pearls Ltd.
    B. North America. United States. Berkeley. University Press
    C. Africa. Cape Town. Justice League
    D. Mexico City. Mexico. Maria Sanchez

26. Under which of the following circumstances would a phonetic filing system be MOST   26._____
effective?

    A. When the person in charge of filing can't spell very well
    B. With large files with names that sound alike
    C. With large files with names that are spelled alike
    D. All of the above

Questions 27-29.

DIRECTIONS: Questions 27 through 29 are to be answered on the basis of the following list
               of numerical files.
        1. 391-023-100
        2. 361-132-170
        3. 385-732-200
        4. 381-432-150
        5. 391-632-387
        6. 361-423-303
        7. 391-123-271

27. Which of the following arrangements of the files follows a consecutive-digit system?   27._____

    A. 2, 3, 4, 1   B. 1, 5, 7, 3
    C. 2, 4, 3, 1   D. 3, 1, 5, 7

28. Which of the following arrangements follows a terminal-digit system?   28._____

    A. 1, 7, 2, 4, 3   B. 2, 1, 4, 5, 7
    C. 7, 6, 5, 4, 3   D. 1, 4, 2, 3, 7

29. Which of the following lists follows a middle-digit system?   29._____

    A. 1, 7, 2, 6, 4, 5, 3   B. 1, 2, 7, 4, 6, 5, 3
    C. 7, 2, 1, 3, 5, 6, 4   D. 7, 1, 2, 4, 6, 5, 3

Questions 30-31.

DIRECTIONS: Questions 30 and 31 are to be answered on the basis of the following informa-
               tion.
      1. Reconfirm Laura Bates appointment with James Caldecort on December 12 at
         9:30 A.M.
      2. Laurence Kinder contact Julia Lucas on August 3 and set up a meeting for week of
         September 23 at 4 P.M.
      3. John Lutz contact Larry Waverly on August 3 and set up appointment for Septem-
         ber 23 at 9:30 A.M.
      4. Call for tickets for Gerry Stanton August 21 for New Jersey on September 23, flight
         143 at 4:43 P.M.

30. A chronological file for the above information would be   30.____

    A. 4, 3, 2, 1   B. 3, 2, 4, 1
    C. 4, 2, 3, 1   D. 3, 1, 2, 4

31. Using the above information, a chronological file for the date of September 23 would be   31.____

    A. 2, 3, 4   B. 3, 1, 4   C. 3, 2, 4   D. 4, 3, 2

Questions 32-34.

DIRECTIONS: Questions 32 through 34 are to be answered on the basis of the following information.

  1. Call Roger Epstein, Ashoke Naipaul, Jon Anderson, and Sarah Washington on April 19 at 1:00 P.M. to set up meeting with Alika D'Ornay for June 6 in New York.
  2. Call Martin Ames before noon on April 19 to confirm afternoon meeting with Bob Greenwood on April 20th
  3. Set up meeting room at noon for 2:30 P.M. meeting on April 19th;
  4. Ashley Stanton contact Bob Greenwood at 9:00 A.M. on April 20 and set up meeting for June 6 at 8:30 A.M.
  5. Carol Guiland contact Shelby Van Ness during afternoon of April 20 and set up meeting for June 6 at 10:00 A.M.
  6. Call airline and reserve tickets on June 6 for Roger Epstein trip *to* Denver on July 8
  7. Meeting at 2:30 P.M. on April 19th

32. A chronological file for all of the above information would be   32.____

    A. 2, 1, 3, 7, 5, 4, 6   B. 3, 7, 2, 1, 4, 5, 6
    C. 3, 7, 1, 2, 5, 4, 6   D. 2, 3, 1, 7, 4, 5, 6

33. A chronological file for the date of April 19th would be   33.____

    A. 2, 3, 7, 1   B. 2, 3, 1, 7
    C. 7, 1, 3, 2   D. 3, 7, 1, 2

34. Add the following information to the file, and then create a chronological file for April 20th: 34.____
    8. April 20: 3:00 P.M. meeting between Bob Greenwood and Martin Ames.

    A. 4, 5, 8   B. 4, 8, 5   C. 8, 5, 4   D. 5, 4, 8

35. The PRIMARY advantage of computer records filing over a manual system is   35.____

    A. speed of retrieval   B. accuracy
    C. cost   D. potential file loss

KEY (CORRECT ANSWERS)

1.	B		16.	B
2.	C		17.	C
3.	D		18.	D
4.	A		19.	A
5.	D		20.	D
6.	C		21.	A
7.	B		22.	B
8.	B		23.	C
9.	C		24.	D
10.	D		25.	A
11.	D		26.	B
12.	C		27.	C
13.	B		28.	D
14.	C		29.	A
15.	D		30.	B

31.	C
32.	D
33.	B
34.	A
35.	A

ARITHMETICAL REASONING
EXAMINATION SECTION
TEST 1

DIRECTIONS: Each question or incomplete statement is followed by several suggested answers or completions. Select the one that BEST answers the question or completes the statement. *PRINT THE LETTER OF THE CORRECT ANSWER IN THE SPACE AT THE RIGHT.*

1. In 2015, a public agency spent $180 to buy pencils that cost three cents each. In 2017, the agency spent $420 to buy the same number of pencils that it had bought in 2015. The price per pencil that the agency paid in 2017 was _____ cents.

   A. 6 1/3　　　B. 2/3　　　C. 7　　　D. 7 3/4

1.____

2. A stenographer spent her 35 hour work week on taking dictation, transcribing the dictated material, and filing.
   If she spent 20% of the work week on taking dictation and 1/2 of the remaining time on transcribing the dictated material, the number of hours of the work week that she spent on filing was

   A. 7　　　B. 10.5　　　C. 14　　　D. 17.5

2.____

3. A typist typed eight pages in two hours.
   If she typed an average of 50 lines per page and an average of 12 words per line, what was her typing speed, in words per minute?

   A. 40　　　B. 50　　　C. 60　　　D. 80

3.____

4. The daily compensation to be paid to each consultant hired in a certain agency is computed by dividing his professional earnings in the previous year by 250. The maximum daily compensation they can receive is $200 each. Four consultants who were hired to work on a special project had the following professional earnings in the previous year: $37,500, $144,000, $46,500, and $61,100. What will be the TOTAL daily cost to the agency for these four consultants?

   A. $932　　　B. $824　　　C. $736　　　D. $712

4.____

5. In a typing and stenographic pool consisting of 30 employees, 2/5 of them are typists, 1/3 of them are senior typists and senior stenographers, and the rest are stenographers.
   If there are 5 more stenographers than senior stenographers, how many senior stenographers are in the typing and stenographic pool?

   A. 3　　　B. 5　　　C. 8　　　D. 10

5.____

6. There are 3,330 copies of a three-page report to be collated. One clerk starts collating at 9:00 A.M. and is joined 15 minutes later by two other clerks. It takes 15 minutes for each of these clerks to collate 90 copies of the report.
   At what time should the job be completed if all three clerks continue working at the same rate without breaks?

   A. 12:00 Noon　　　　　B. 12:15 P.M.
   C. 1:00 P.M.　　　　　　D. 1:15 P.M.

6.____

7. By the end of last year, membership in the blood credit program in a certain agency had increased from the year before by 500, bringing the total to 2,500.
If the membership increased by the same percentage this year, the TOTAL number of members in the blood credit program for this agency by the end of this year should be

    A. 2,625   B. 3,000   C. 3,125   D. 3,250

7.___

8. During this year, an agency suggestion program put into practice suggestions from 24 employees, thereby saving the agency 40 times the amount of money it paid in awards. If 1/3 of the employees were awarded $50 each, 1/2 of the employees were awarded $25 each, and the rest were awarded $10 each, how much money did the agency save by using the suggestions?

    A. $18,760   B. $29,600   C. C, $32,400   D. $46,740

8.___

9. A senior stenographer earned $20,100 a year and had 4.5% state tax withheld for the year.
If she was paid every two weeks, the amount of state tax that was taken out of each of her paychecks, based on a 52-week year, was MOST NEARLY

    A. $31.38   B. $32.49   C. $34.77   D. $36.99

9.___

10. Two stenographers have been assigned to address 750 envelopes. One stenographer addresses twice as many envelopes per hour as the other stenographer.
If it takes five hours for them to complete the job, the rate of the slower stenographer is _____ envelopes per hour.

    A. 35   B. 50   C. 75   D. 100

10.___

11. Suppose that the postage rate for mailing single copies of a magazine to persons not included on a subscription list is 18 cents for the first two ounces of the single copy and 3 cents for each additional ounce.
If 19 copies of a magazine, each of which weighs eleven ounces, are mailed to 19 different people, the TOTAL postage cost of these magazines is

    A. $3.42   B. $3.99   C. $6.18   D. $8.55

11.___

12. A senior stenographer spends about 40 hours a month taking dictation. Of that time, 44% is spent taking minutes of meetings, 38% is spent taking dictation of lengthy reports, and the rest of the time is spent taking dictation of letters and memoranda.
How much MORE time is spent taking minutes of meetingsthan in taking dictation of letters and memoranda?
10 hours _____ minutes.

    A. 6   B. 16   C. 24   D. 40

12.___

13. In one week, a stenographer typed 65 letters. Forty letters had 4 copies on colored paper. The rest had 3 copies on colored paper.
If the stenographer had 500 sheets of colored paper on hand at the beginning of the week when she started typing the letters, how many sheets of colored paper did she have left at the end of the week?

    A. 190   B. 235   C. 265   D. 305

13.___

14. An agency is planning to microfilm letters and other correspondence of the last five years. The number of letter-size documents that can be photographed on a 100-foot roll of microfilm is 2,995. The agency estimates that it will need 240 feet of microfilm to do all the pages of all of the letters.
How many pages of letter-size documents can be photographed on this microfilm?

    A. 5,990   B. 6,786   C. 7,188   D. 7,985

14.____

15. In an agency, 2/3 of the total number of female stenographers and 1/2 of the total number of male stenographers attended a general staff meeting.
If there are a total of 56 stenographers in the agency and 25% of them are male, the number of female stenographers who attended the general staff meeting is

    A. 14   B. 28   C. 36   D. 42

15.____

16. A worker is currently earning $17,140 a year and pays $350 a month for rent. He expects to get a raise that will enable him to move into an apartment where his rent will be 25% of his new yearly salary.
If this new apartment is going to cost him $390 a month, what is the TOTAL amount of raise that he expects to get?

    A. $480   B. $980   C. $1,580   D. $1,840

16.____

17. The tops of five desks in an office are to be covered with a scratch-resistant material. Each desk top measures 60 inches by 36 inches.
How many square feet of material will be needed for the five desk tops?

    A. 15   B. 75   C. 96   D. 180

17.____

18. Three grades of bond paper are used in a central transcribing unit. The cost per ream of paper is $1.90 for Grade A, $1.70 for Grade B, and $1.60 for Grade C.
If the central transcribing unit used 6 reams of Grade A paper, 14 reams of Grade B paper, and 20 reams of Grade C paper, the AVERAGE cost, per ream, of the bond paper used by this unit is between

    A. $1.62 and $1.66   B. $1.66 and $1.70
    C. $1.70 and $1.74   D. $1.74 and $1.80

18.____

19. The Complaint Bureau of a city agency is composed of an investigation unit, a clerical unit, and a central transcribing unit. The sum of $264,000 has been appropriated for the operation of this bureau. Of this sum, $170,000 is to be allotted to the clerical unit.
Of this bureau's total appropriation, the percentage that is left for the central transcribing unit is MOST NEARLY ____ if $41,200 is allotted for investigations.

    A. 20%   B. 30%   C. 40%   D. 50%

19.____

20. Three typists were assigned to address a total of 2,655 postcards. Typist A addressed the postcards at the rate of 170 per hour. Typist B addressed the postcards at the rate of 150 per hour. Typist C's rate is not known. After the three typists had addressed postcards for three and a half hours, Typist C was taken off this assignment. It was necessary for Typist A and Typist B to work two and a half hours more to complete this assignment. The rate per hour at which Typist C addressed the postcards was

20.____

A. less than 150
B. between 150 and 170
C. more than 170 but less than 200
D. more than 200

21. In 2015, a city agency bought 12,000 envelopes at $4.00 per hundred. In 2016, the price of envelopes purchased was 40 percent higher than the 2010 price, but only 60 percent as many envelopes were bought.
The total cost of the envelopes purchased in 2016 was MOST NEARLY

    A. $250   B. $320   C. $400   D. $480

21.____

22. A stenographer has been assigned to place entries on 500 forms. She places entries on 25 forms by the end of half an hour, when she is joined by another stenographer. The second stenographer places entries at the rate of 45 an hour.
Assuming that both stenographers continue to work at their respective rates of speed, the TOTAL number of hours required to carry out the entire assignment is

    A. 5   B. 54   C. 64   D. 7

22.____

23. On Monday, a stenographer took dictation without interruption for 1 1/2 hours and transcribed all the dictated material in 3 1/2 hours. On Tuesday, she took dictation uninterruptedly for 1 3/4 hours and transcribed all the material in 3 3/4 hours. On Wednesday, she took dictation without interruption for 2 1/4 hours and transcribed all the material in 4 1/2 hours.
If she took dictation at the average rate of 90 words per minute during these three days, then her average transcription rate, in words per minute, for the same three days was MOST NEARLY

    A. 36   B. 41   C. 54   D. 58

23.____

24. In a division of clerks and stenographers, 15 people are currently employed, 20% of whom are stenographers.
If management plans are to maintain the current number of stenographers, but to increase the clerical staff to the point where 12% of the total staff are stenographers, what is the MAXIMUM number of additional clerks that should be hired to meet these plans?

    A. 3   B. 8   C. 10   D. 12

24.____

25. In the first quarter of the year, a certain operator sent out 230 quarterly reports. In the second quarter of that year, he sent out 310 quarterly reports.
The percent increase in the number of quarterly reports he sent out in the second quarter of the year compared to the first quarter of the year is MOST NEARLY

    A. 26%   B. 29%   C. 35%   D. 39%

25.____

KEY (CORRECT ANSWERS)

1.	C		11.	D
2.	C		12.	C
3.	A		13.	C
4.	C		14.	C
5.	A		15.	B
6.	B		16.	C
7.	C		17.	B
8.	B		18.	B
9.	C		19.	A
10.	B		20.	D

21.	C
22.	B
23.	B
24.	C
25.	C

———

SOLUTIONS TO PROBLEMS

1. $180 ÷ .03 = 6000 pencils bought. In 2017, the price per pencil = $420 / 6000 = .07 = 7 cents.

2. Number of hours on filing = 35 - (.20)(35) - (1/2)(28) = 14

3. Eight pages contains (8)(50)(12) = 4800 words. She thus typed 4800 words in 120 minutes = 40 words per minute.

4. $37,500 ÷ 250 = $150; $144,000 ÷ 250 = $576; $46,500 ÷ 250 = $186; $61,100 ÷ 250 = $244.40 Since $200 = maximum compensation for any single consultant, total compensation = $150 + $200 + $186 + $200 = $736

5. Number of typists = (2/5)(30) = 12, number of senior typists and senior stenographers = (1/3)(30) = 10, number of stenographers = 30 - 12 - 10 = 8. Finally, number of senior stenographers = 8-5 = 3

6. At 9:15 AM, 90 copies have been collated. The remaining 3240 copies are being collated at the rate of (3)(90) = 270 every 15 minutes = 1080 per hour. Since 3240 ÷ 1080 = 3 hours, the clerks will finish at 9:15 AM + 3 hours = 12:15 PM.

7. During last year, the membership increased from 2000 to 2500, which represents a (500/2000)(100) = 25% increase. A 25% increase during this year means the membership = (2500)(1.25) = 3125

8. Total awards = (1/3)(24)($50) + (1/2)(24)($25) + (1/6)(24)($10) = $740. Thus, the savings = (40)($740) = $29,600

9. Her pay for 2 weeks = $20,100 ÷ 26 ≈ $773.08. Thus, her state tax for 2 weeks ≈ ($773.08)(.045) ≈ $34.79. (Nearest correct answer is $34.77 in four selections.)

10. 750 ÷ 5 hours = 150 envelopes per hour for the 2 stenographers combined. Let x = number of envelopes addressed by the slower stenographer . Then, x + 2x = 150. Solving, x = 50

11. Total cost = (19)[.18+(.03)(9)] = $8.55

12. (.44)(40) - (.18)(40) = 10.4 hrs. = 10 hrs. 24 rain.

13. 500 - (40)(4) - (25)(3) = 265

14. 2995 ÷ 100 = 29.95 documents per foot of microfilm roll. Then, (29.95)(240 ft) = 7188 documents

15. There are (.75)(56) = 42 female stenographers. Then, (2/3)(42) = 28 of them attended the meeting.

16. ($390)(12) = $4680 new rent per year. Then, ($4680)(4) = $18,720 = his new yearly salary. His raise = $18,720 - $17,140 = $1580

17. Number of sq.ft. = (5)(60)(36) ÷ 144 = 75

18. Average cost per ream = [($1.90)(6) + ($1.70) (14) + ($1.60) (20)] / 40 = $1.68, which is between $1.66 and $1.70

19. $264,000 - $170,000 - $41,200 = 52,800 = 20%

20. Let x = typist C's rate. Since typists A and B each worked 6 hrs., while typist C worked only 3.5 hrs., we have (6)(170) + (6)(150) + 3.5x = 2655. Solving, x = 210, which is nore than 200.

21. In 2016, the cost per hundred envelopes was ($4.00)(1.40) = $5.60 and (.60)(12,000) = 7200 envelopes were bought. Total cost in 2016 = (72)($5.60) = $403.20, or about $400.

22. The 1st stenographer's rate is 50 forms per hour. After 1/2 hr., there are 500 - 25 = 475 forms to be done and the combined rate of the 2 stenographers is 95 forms per hr. Thus, total hrs. required = 1/2 + (475) ÷ (95) = 5 1/2

23. Total time for dictation = 1 1/4 + 1 3/4 + 2 1/4 = 5 1/4 hrs. = 315 min. The number of words = (90)(315) = 28,350. The total transcription 3 time = 3 1/4 + 3 3/4 + 44 = 11 1/2 hrs. = 690 min. Her average transcription rate

= 28,350 ÷ 690 ≈ 41 words per min.

24. Currently, there are (.20)(15) = 3 stenographers, and thus 12 clerks. Let x = additional clerks. Then, $\frac{3}{3+12+x}$ = .12. This simplifies to 3 = (.12)(15+x). Solving, x = 10

25. Percent increase = ($\frac{80}{230}$)(100) ≈ 35%

TEST 2

DIRECTIONS: Each question or incomplete statement is followed by several suggested answers or completions. Select the one that BEST answers the question or completes the statement. *PRINT THE LETTER OF THE CORRECT ANSWER IN THE SPACE AT THE RIGHT.*

1. A school has 112 homeroom classes. There were 15 school days in February. The aggregate register of the school for the month of February was 52,920; the aggregate attendance was 43,860.
    The average class size, to the NEAREST tenth, is

    A. 35.3   B. 31.5   C. 29.2   D. 26.9

    1.____

2. As the school secretary in charge of supplies, you are asked to order the following items on a supplementary requisition for general supplies:
    5 gross of red pencils at $8.90 per dozen
    5,000 manila envelopes at $2.35 per C
    36 rulers at $187.20 per gross
    6 boxes of manila paper at $307.20 per carton (24 boxes to a carton)
    180 reams of composition paper at $27.80 per carton (20 reams to a carton)
    The TOTAL amount of the order is

    A. $957.20   B. $1,025.30   C. $916.80   D. $991.30

    2.____

3. In the high school to which you have been assigned as a school secretary, the annual allotment for general supplies, textbooks, repairs, etc. for the school year 2015-16 was $37,500. A special allotment of $10,000 was granted for textbooks ordered from the State Textbook List. The original requisition for general and vocational supplies amounted to $12,514.75; for science supplies, $6,287.25; for textbooks, including the special funds, $13,785.00; monies spent for equipment repairs and science perishables through December 31, 2015, $1,389.68.
    The balance in your supply allotment account on January 1, 2016 will be

    A. $14,913.00   B. $13,523.32
    C. $17,308.32   D. $3,523.32

    3.____

4. The teacher of one of the sixth term typing classes in the high school to which you are assigned as a school secretary has agreed to have her students type attendance cards for the incoming students for the new school year, commencing in September, as a work project. There are 24 students in the class; each student can complete 8 cards during a typing period. There will be 4,032 new students in September.
    The number of typing periods required to complete the task is

    A. 31   B. 21   C. 28   D. 24

    4.____

5. As a school secretary assigned to payroll duties, you are required to prepare the extra-curricular payroll report for the coaches teams in your high school. The rate of pay for these activities was increased on November 1 from $148 per session to $174.50 per session. The pay period which you are reporting is for the months of October, November, and December. Mr. Jones, the football coach, conducted 15 practice sessions in October, 20 in November, and 30 in December.
    His TOTAL gross pay on the December extra-curricular payroll report is

    5.____

A. $10,547.50
C. $10,945.00

B. $10,415.00
D. $11,342.50

6.   The comparative results on a uniform examination given in your school for the last three   6.____
     years follow:

	2014	2015	2016
Number taking test	501	496	485
Number passing test	441	437	436

The percentage of passing, to the nearest tenth of a percent, for the year in which the
HIGHEST percent of students passed is

A.   89.3%   B.   88%   C.   89.9%   D.   90.3%

7.   During his first seven terms in high school, a student compiled the following averages: 7.____

Term	Numbers of Majors Completed	Average
1	4	81.25%
2	4	83.75%
3	5	86.2%
4	5	85.8%
5	5	87.0%
6	5	83.4%
7	5	82.6%

In his eighth term, the student had the following final marks in major subjects: 90%, 95%,
80%, 90%, 85%. The student's average for all eight terms of high school, correct to the
nearest tenth of a percent, is

A.   84.8%   B.   84.7%   C.   84.9%   D.   85.8%

8.   A secretary is asked by her employer to order an office machine which lists at a price of   8.____
     $360, less trade discounts of 20% and 10%, terms 2/10, n/30. There is a delivery charge
     of $8 and an installation charge of $12. If the machine is paid for in 10 days, the TOTAL
     cost of the machine will be

A. $264.80   B. $258.40   C. $266.96   D. $274.02

9.   The school to which you have been assigned as school secretary has an annual allow-   9.____
     ance of 5,120 hours for all teacher aides. The principal decides to employ 5 teacher
     aides from 8:00 A.M. to 12:00 Noon, and 5 other teacher aides from 12:00 Noon to 4:00
     P.M. daily for as many days as his allowance permits.
     If a teacher aide earns $17.00 an hour, and he is present every day, his TOTAL earn-
     ings for the school year will be more than

     A. $7,000 but less than $8,000
     B. $8,000 but less than $9,000
     C. $9,000 but less than $10,000
     D. $10,000

10. During examination week in a high school to which you have been assigned as school secretary, teachers are required to be in school at least 6 hours and 20 minutes daily although their arrival and departure times may vary each day. A teacher's time card that you have been asked to check shows the following entries for the week of June 17:

Date	Arrival	Departure
17	7:56 AM	2:18 PM
18	9:53 AM	4:22 PM
19	12:54 PM	7:03 PM
20	9:51 AM	4:15 PM
21	7:58 AM	2:11 PM

During the week of June 17 to June 21, the teacher was in school for AT LEAST the minimum required time on _____ days.

A. 2 of the 5 B. 3 of the 5
C. 4 of the 5 D. all 5

10.___

11. As school secretary, you are asked to find the total of the following bill received in your school:
   750 yellow envelopes at $.22 per C
   2,400 white envelopes at $2.80 per M
   30 rulers at $5.04 per gross
The TOTAL of the bill is

A. $69.90 B. $24.27 C. $18.87 D. $9.42

11.___

12. A department in the school to which you have been assigned as school secretary has been given a textbook allowance of $5,500 for the school year. The department's textbook order is:
   75 books at $32.50 each
   45 books at $49.50 each
   25 books at $34.50 each
The TOTAL of the department's order is _____ the allowance.

A. $27.50 over B. $27.50 under
C. $72.50 under D. $57.50 over

12.___

13. The total receipts, including 5% city sales tax, for the G.O. store for the first week of school amounted to $489.09.
The receipts from the G.O. store for the first week of school, excluding the 5% city sales tax, amounted to

A. $465.80 B. $464.64 C. $464.63 D. $513.54

13.___

14. Class sizes in the school to which you have been assigned as school secretary are as follows:

Number of Classes	Class Size
9	29 pupils
12	31 pupils
15	32 pupils
7	33 pupils
11	34 pupils

The average class size in this school, correct to the nearest tenth, is

A. 30.8 B. 31.9 C. 31.8 D. 30.9

14.___

15. In 2013, the social security tax was 4.2% for the first $6,600 earned a year. In 2014, the social security tax was 4.4% on the first $6,600 earned a year.
For a teacher aide earning $19,200 in 2013 and $20,400 in 2014, the increase in social security tax deduction in 2014 over 2013 was

    A. $132.00   B. $13.20   C. $19.20   D. $20.40

15.____

16. A teacher aide earning $23,900 a year will incur automatic deductions of 3.90% for social security and .50% for medicare, based on the first $6,600 a year earnings. The TOTAL tax deduction for these two items will be

    A. $274   B. $290.40   C. $525.80   D. $300.40

16.____

17. The school store turns in receipts totaling $131.25 to the school treasurer, including 5% which has been collected for sales tax.
The amount of money which the treasurer MUST set aside for sales tax is

    A. $6.56   B. $6.25   C. $5.00   D. $5.25

17.____

18. One of the custodial assistants can wash all the windows in the main office in 3 hours. A second assistant can wash the windows in the main office in 2 hours.
If the two men work together, they should complete the task in _____ hour(s) _____ minutes.

    A. 1; 0   B. 1.5; 0   C. 1; 12   D. 1; 15

18.____

19. A school secretary is requested by the principal to order an office machine which lists at a price of $120, less discounts of 10% and 5%.
The net price of the machine to the school will be

    A. $100.50   B. $102.00   C. $102.60   D. $103.00

19.____

20. Five students are employed at school under a work-study program through which they are paid $10.00 an hour for work in school offices, but no student may earn more than $450 a month. Three days before the end of the month, you note that the student payroll totals $2,062.50.
The number of hours which each of the students may work during the remainder of the month is_____hour(s).

    A. 4   B. 2   C. 1   D. 3

20.____

21. You are asked to summarize expenditures made by the school within the budget allocation for the school year. You determine that the following expenditures have been made: educational supplies, $2,600; postage, $650; emergency repairs, $225; textbooks, $5,100; instructional equipment, $1,200.
Since $10,680 has been allocated to the school, the following sum still remains available for office supplies:

    A. $905   B. $1,005   C. $800   D. $755

21.____

22. In preparing the percentage of attendance for the period report, you note that the aggregate attendance is 57,585 and the aggregate register is 62,000.
The percentage of attendance, to the nearest tenth of a percent, is

    A. 91.9%   B. 93.0%   C. 92.8%   D. 92.9%

22.___

23. You borrow $1,200 from your retirement fund which you must repay over a period of three years, with interest of $144, each payment to be divided equally among 36 total payments.
The monthly deduction from your paycheck will be

    A. $37.33   B. $36.00   C. $33.00   D. $37.30

23.___

24. Tickets for a school dance are printed, starting with number 401 and ending with number 1650. They are to be sold for 75¢ each. The tickets remaining unsold should start with number 1569.
The amount of cash which should be collected for the sale of tickets is

    A. $876.75   B. $937.50   C. $876.00   D. $875.25

24.___

25. Stage curtains are purchased by the school and delivered on October 3 under terms of 5/10, 2/30, net/60. The curtains are paid in full by a check for $522.50 on October 12.
The invoice price was

    A. $533.16   B. $522.50   C. $540.00   D. $550.00

25.___

———

KEY (CORRECT ANSWERS)

1.	B	11.	D
2.	B	12.	A
3.	B	13.	A
4.	B	14.	C
5.	C	15.	B
6.	C	16.	B
7.	C	17.	B
8.	D	18.	C
9.	B	19.	C
10.	B	20.	D

21.	A
22.	D
23.	A
24.	C
25.	D

SOLUTIONS TO PROBLEMS

1. Average class size = 52,920 ÷ 15 ÷ 112 = 31.5

2. Total amount = (5)(12)($8.90) + (50)($2.35) + (36) ($187.20) ÷ 144 + (6)($307.20) ÷ 24 + (9)($27.80) = $1025.30

3. Balance = $37,500 + $10,000 - $12,514.75 - $6287.25 - $13,785 - $1389.68 = $13,523.32

4. (24)(8) = 192 cards completed in one period. Then, 4032 ÷ 192 = 21 typing periods required.

5. Total pay = (15)($148.00) + (20)($174.50) + (30)($174.50) = $10,945.00

6. The passing rates for 2014, 2015, 2016 were 88.0%, 88.1%, and 89.9%, respectively. So, 89.9% was the highest.

7. His 8th term average was 88.0%. His overall average for all 8 terms = [(4)(81.25%)+(4)(83.75%)+(5)(86.2%)+(5)(85.8%)+ (5)(87.0%)+(5)(83.4%)+(5)(82.6%)+(5)(88.0%)] ÷ 38 = 84.9%

8. Total cost = ($360)(.80)(.90)(.98) + $8 + $12 ≈ $274.02 (Exact amount = $274.016)

9. 5120 ÷ 4 = 1280 teacher-days. Then, 1280 ÷ 10 = 128 days per teacher. A teacher's earnings for these 128 days = ($17.00)(4)(128)= $8704, which is more than $8000 but less than $9000.

10. The number of hours present on each of the 5 days listed was 6 hrs. 22 min., 6 hrs. 29 min., 6 hrs. 9 min., 6 hrs. 24 min., and 6 hrs. 13 min. On 3 days, he met the minimum time.

11. Total cost = (7.5)(.22) + (2.4)($2.80) + (30/144)(5.04) = $9.42

12. Textbook order = (75)($32.50) + (45)($49.50) + (25)($34.50) = $5527.50, which is $27.50 over the allowance.

13. Receipts without the tax = $489.09 ÷ 1.05 = $465.80

14. Average class size = [(9)(29)+(12)(31)+(7)(33)+(11)(34)+(15)(32)] ÷ 54 ≈ 31.8

15. ($6600)(.044-.042) = $13.20

16. ($6600)(.039+.005) = $290.40

17. $131.25 = 1.05x, x = 125, $131.25 - 125.00 = 6.25

18. Let x = hours needed working together. Then, (1/3)(x) + (1/2)(x) = 1
     Simplifying, 2x + 3x = 6. Solving, x = 1 1/5 hrs. = 1 hr. 12 min.

19. Net price = 120 - 10% (12) = 108; 108 - 5% (5.40) = 102.60

20. ($225)(5) - $1031.25 = $93.75 remaining in the month. Since the 5 students earn
     $25 per hour combined, $93.75 ÷ $25 = 3.75, which must be rounded down to 3
     hours.

21. $10,680 - $2600 - $650 - $225 - $5100 - $1200 = $905 for office supplies.

22.   57,585 ÷ 62,000 ≈ .9288 ≈ 92.9%

23. Monthly deduction = $1344 ÷ 36 = $37.33 (Technically, 35 payments of $37.33
     and 1 payment of $37.45)

24. (1569-401)(.75) = $876.00

25. The invoice price (which reflects the 5% discount) is $522.50 ÷ .95 = $550.00

———————

TEST 3

DIRECTIONS: Each question or incomplete statement is followed by several suggested answers or completions. Select the one that BEST answers the question or completes the statement. *PRINT THE LETTER OF THE CORRECT ANSWER IN THE SPACE AT THE RIGHT.*

1. If an inch on an office layout drawing equals 4 feet of actual floor dimension, then a room which actually measures 9 feet by 14 feet is represented on the drawing by measurements equaling _____ inches x _____ inches.

   A. 2 1/4; 3 1/2   B. 2 1/2; 3 1/2   C. 2 1/4;3 1/4   D. 2 1/2;3 1/4

   1.___

2. A cooperative education intern works from 1:30 P.M. to 5 P.M. on Mondays, Wednesdays, and Fridays, and from 10 A.M. to 2:30 P.M. with no lunch hour on Tuesdays and Thursdays. He earns $13.50 an hour on this job. In addition, he has a Saturday job paying $16.00 an hour at which he works from 9 A.M. to 3 P.M. with a half hour off for lunch. The gross amount that the student earns each week is MOST NEARLY

   A. $321.90   B. $355.62   C. $364.02   D. $396.30

   2.___

3. Thirty-five percent of the College Discovery students who entered community college earned an associate degree. Of these students, 89% entered senior college, of which 67% went on to earn baccalaureate degrees.
   If there were 529 College Discovery students who entered community college, then the number of those who went on to finally receive a baccalaureate degree is MOST NEARLY

   A. 354   B. 315   C. 124   D. 110

   3.___

4. It takes 5 office assistants two days to type 125 letters. Each of the assistants works at an equal rate of speed. How many days will it take 10 office assistants to type 200 letters?

   A. 1   B. 1 3/5   C. 2   D. 2 1/5

   4.___

5. The following are the grades and credits earned by Student X during the first two years in college.

Grade	Credits	Weight	Quality Points
A	10 1/2	x4	
B	24	x3	
C	12	x2	
D	4 1/2	x1	
F, FW	5	x0	

   To compute an index number:
   I.   Multiply the number of credits of each grade by the weight to get the number of *quality points.*
   II. Add the credits.
   III. Add the quality points.
   IV. Divide the total quality points by the total credits, and carry the division to two decimal places.

   On the basis of the given information, the index number for Student X is

   A. 2.54   B. 2.59   C. 2.63   D. 2.68

   5.___

6. Typist X can type 20 forms per hour, and Typist Y can type 30 forms per hour. If there are   6._____
   30 forms to be typed and both typists are put to work on the job, how soon should they be
   expected to finish the work?
   _____ minutes.

   A.   32   B.   34   C.   36   D.   38

7. Assume that there were 18 working days in February and that the six clerks in your unit   7._____
   had the following number of absences:

Clerk	Absences
F	3
G	2
H	8
I	1
J	0
K	5

   The average percentage attendance for the six clerks in your unit in February was MOST
   NEARLY

   A.   80%   B.   82%   C.   84%   D.   86%

8. A certain employee is paid at the rate of $7.50 per hour, with time and a half for overtime.   8._____
   Hours in excess of 40 hours a week count as overtime. During the past week, the
   employee put in 48 working hours. The employee's gross wages for the week are MOST
   NEARLY

   A. $330   B. $350   C. $370   D. $390

9. You are making a report on the number of inside and outside calls handled by a particu-   9._____
   lar switchboard. Over a 15-day period, the total number of all inside and outside calls
   handled by the switchboard was 5,760. The average number of inside calls per day was
   234. You cannot find one day's tally of outside calls, but the total number of outside calls
   for the other fourteen days was 2,065. From this information, how many outside calls
   must have been reported on the missing tally?

   A.   175   B.   185   C.   195   D.   205

10. A floor plan has been prepared for a new building, drawn to a scale of 3/4 inch = 1 foot.   10._____
    A certain area is drawn 1 and 1/2 feet long and 6 inches wide on the floor plan. What are
    the ACTUAL dimensions of this area in the new building?
    _____ feet long and _____ feet wide.

    A.   21; 8   B.   24; 8   C.   27; 9   D.   30; 9

11. You are preparing a package of six books to mail to a professor who is on sabbatical.   11._____
    They weigh, respectively, 1 pound 11 ounces, 1 pound 6 ounces, 2 pounds 1 ounce, 2
    pounds 2 ounces, 1 pound 7 ounces, and 1 pound 8 ounces. The packaging material
    weighs 6 ounces.
    The TOTAL weight of the package will be_____ pounds _____ ounces.

    A.   10; 3   B.   10; 9   C.   11; 5   D.   12; 5

12. Part-time students are charged $70 per credit for courses at a particular college. In addition, they must pay a $24.00 student activity fee if they take six credits or more and $14.00 lab fee for each laboratory course.
If a person takes one 3-credit course and one 4-credit course and his 4-credit course is a laboratory course, the TOTAL cost to him will be

   A. $504　　　　B. $528　　　　C. $542　　　　D. $552

12.___

13. The graduating class of a certain community college consisted of 378 majors in secretarial science, 265 majors in engineering science, 57 majors in nursing, 513 majors in accounting, and 865 majors in liberal arts.
The percent of students who major in liberal arts at this college was MOST NEARLY

   A.   24.0%　　　　B.   41.6%　　　　C.   52.3%　　　　D.   71.6%

13.___

14. Donald Smith earns $12.80 an hour for forty hours a week, with time and a half for all hours over forty. Last week, his total earnings amounted to $627.20.
He worked_____ hours.

   A.   46　　　　B.   47　　　　C.   48　　　　D.   49

14.___

15. Mr. Jones desires to sell an article costing $28 at a gross profit of 30% of the selling price, and to allow a trade discount of 20% of the list price.
The list price of the article should be

   A. $43.68　　　　B. $45.50　　　　C. $48.00　　　　D. $50.00

15.___

16. The gauge of an oil storage tank in an elementary school indicates 1/5 full. After a truck delivers 945 gallons of oil, the gauge indicates 4/5 full.
The capacity of the tank is _____ gallons.

   A.   1,260　　　　B.   1,575　　　　C.   1,625　　　　D.   1,890

16.___

17. An invoice dated April 3, terms 3/10, 2/30, net/60, was paid in full with a check for $787.92 on May 1.
The amount of the invoice was

   A. $772.16　　　　B. $787.92　　　　C. $804.00　　　　D. $812.29

17.___

18. Two pipes supply the water for the swimming pool at Blenheim High School. One pipe can fill the pool in 9 hours. The second pipe can fill the pool in 6 hours.
If both pipes were opened simultaneously, the pool could be filled in _____ hours minutes.

   A.   3; 36　　　　B.   4; 30　　　　C.   5; 15　　　　D.   7; 30

18.___

19. John's father spent $24,000, which was one-fourth of his savings. He bought a car with three-eighths of the remainder of his savings.
His bank balance now amounts to

   A. $30,000　　　　B. $32,000　　　　C. $45,000　　　　D. $50,000

19.___

20. A clock that loses 4 minutes every 24 hours was set at 6 A.M. on October 1. What time was indicated by the clock when the CORRECT time was 12:00 Noon on October 6th?
    _____ A.M.

    A. 11:36   B. 11:38   C. 11:39   D. 11:40

20._____

21. Unit S's production fluctuated substantially from one year to another. In 2009, Unit S's production was 100% greater than in 2008. In 2010, production decreased by 25% from 2009. In 2011, Unit S's production was 10% greater than in 2010. On the basis of this information, it is CORRECT to conclude that Unit S's production in 2011 exceeded Unit S's production in 2008 by

    A. 65%   B. 85%   C. 95%   D. 135%

21._____

22. Agency X is moving into a new building. It has 1,500 employees presently on its staff and does not contemplate much variance from this level. The new building contains 100 available offices, each with a maximum capacity of 30 employees. It has been decided that only 2/3 of the maximum capacity of each office will be utilized. The TOTAL number of offices that will be occupied by Agency X is

    A. 30   B. 66   C. 75   D. 90

22._____

23. One typist completes a form letter every 5 minutes and another typist completes one every 6 minutes. If the two typists start together, how many minutes later will they again start typing new letters simultaneously and how many letters will they have completed by that time?
    _____ minutes - _____ letters.

    A. 11; 30   B. 12; 24   C. 24; 12   D. 30; 1

23._____

24. During one week, a machine operator produces 10 fewer pages per hour of work than he usually does.
    If it ordinarily takes him six hours to produce a 300-page report, how many hours LONGER will that same 300-page report take him during the week when he produces more slowly?
    _____ hours longer.

    A. 1 1/2   B. 1 2/3   C. 2   D. 2 3/4

24._____

25. A study reveals that Miss Brown files N cards in M hours, and Miss Smith files the same number of cards in T hours. If the two employees work together, the number of hours it will take them to file N cards is

25._____

A. $\dfrac{N}{\dfrac{N}{M} + \dfrac{N}{N}}$

B. $\dfrac{N}{T + M} + \dfrac{2N}{MT}$

C. $N\left(\dfrac{M}{N} + \dfrac{N}{T}\right)$

D. $\dfrac{N}{NT + MN}$

KEY (CORRECT ANSWERS)

1.	A		11.	B
2.	B		12.	B
3.	D		13.	B
4.	B		14.	A
5.	A		15.	D
6.	C		16.	B
7.	B		17.	C
8.	D		18.	A
9.	B		19.	C
10.	B		20.	C

21.	A
22.	C
23.	D
24.	A
25.	A

———

SOLUTIONS TO PROBLEMS

1. 9/4 = 2 1/4" and 14/4 = 3 1/2"

2. Gross amount = (3)($6.75)(3.5) + (2)($6.75)(4.5) + ($8.00)(5.5) = $175.625, which is closest to selection B ($177.81).

3. $(529)(.35)(.89)(.67) \approx 110$

4. 10 worker-days are needed to type 125 letters, so (200)(10) ÷ 125 = 16 worker-days are needed to type 200 letters. Finally, 16 ÷ 10 workers = 1 3/5 days.

5. Index number = [(14)(10 1/2) + (3) (24) + (2) (12) + (1)(4 1/2) +

   (0)(5)] ÷ 56 $\approx$ 2.54

6. Typist X could do 30 forms in 30/20 = 1 1/2 hours. Let x = number of hours needed when working together with typist Y.

   Then, $(\frac{1}{1\frac{1}{2}})(x)+(\frac{1}{1})x=1$. Simplifying, 2x+3x=3, so $x=\frac{3}{5}$hr.= 36 min.

7. $(3+2+8+1+0+5) \div 6 = 3.1\overline{6}$. Then, $18 \sim 3.\overline{6} = 14.8\overline{3}$.

   Finally, $14.8\overline{3} \div 18 \approx 82\%$

8. Wages = ($7.50)(40) + ($11.25)(8) = $390

9. (234)(15) = 3510 inside calls. Then, 5760 - 3510 = 2250 outside calls. Finally, 2250 - 2065 = 185 outside calls on the missing day.

10. 18 ÷ 3/4 = 24 feet long and 6 ÷ 3/4 = 8 feet wide.

11. Total weight = 1 lb. 11 oz. + 1 lb. 6 oz. + 2 lbs. 1 oz. + 2 lbs. 2 oz + 1 lb. 7 oz. + 1 lb. 8 oz. + 6 oz. = 8 lbs. 41 oz. = 10 lbs. 9 oz.

12. Total cost = ($70)(7) + $24 + $14 = $528

13. 865 ÷ 2078 $\approx$ 41.6% liberal arts majors

14. ($12.80)(40)= $512, so he made $627.20 - $512 = $115.20 in overtime. His overtime rate = ($12.80)(1.5)= $19.20 per hour. Thus, he worked $115.20 ÷ $19.20 = 6 overtime hours. Total hours worked =46.

15. Let x = list price. Selling price = .80x. Then, .80x - (.30)(.80x) = $28. Simplifying, .56x = $28. Solving, x = $50.00

16. 945 gallons represents $\frac{4}{5} - \frac{1}{5} = \frac{3}{5}$ of the tank's capacity. Then, the capacity

    $= 945 \div \frac{3}{5} = 1575$ gallons

17. $787.92 ÷ .98 = $804.00

18. Let x = number of required hours. Then, (1/9)(x) + (1/6)(x) = 1 Simplifying, 2x + 3x = 18. Solving, x = 3.6 hours = 3 hrs. 36 min.

19. Bank balance = $96,000 - $24,000 - (3/8) ($72,000) = $45,000

20. From Oct. 1, 6 AM to Oct. 6, Noon = 5 1/2 days. The clock would show a loss of (4 min.)(5 1/2) = 21 min. Thus, the clock's time would (incorrectly) show 12:00 Noon - 21 min. = 11:39 AM

21. 2008 = x, 2009 = 200x, 2010 = 150x, 2011 = 165x
    65% more

22. (2/3)(30) = 20 employees in each office. Then, 1500 ÷ 20 = 75 offices

23. After 30 minutes, the typists will have finished a total of 6 + 5 = 11 letters.

24. When he works more slowly, he will only produce 300 - (6)(10) = 240 pages in 6 hrs. His new slower rate is 40 pages per hour, so he will need 60/40 = 1 1/2 more hours to do the remaining 60 pages.

25. Let x = required hours. Then, $(\frac{1}{M})(x) + (\frac{1}{T})(x) = 1$. Simplifying, , x(T+M) = MT. Solving, x = MT/(T+M).
    Note: The N value is immaterial. Also, choice A reduces to MT/(T+M).

READING COMPREHENSION
UNDERSTANDING AND INTERPRETING WRITTEN MATERIAL
EXAMINATION SECTION
TEST 1

DIRECTIONS: Each question or incomplete statement is followed by several suggested answers or completions. Select the one that BEST answers the question or completes the statement. *PRINT THE LETTER OF THE CORRECT ANSWER IN THE SPACE AT THE RIGHT.*

Questions 1-3.

DIRECTIONS: Questions 1 through 3 are to be answered SOLELY on the basis of the following statement.

The equipment in a mailroom may include a mail metering machine. This machine simultaneously stamps, postmarks, seals, and counts letters as fast as the operator can feed them. It can also print the proper postage directly on a gummed strip to be affixed to bulky items. It is equipped with a meter which is removed from the machine and sent to the postmaster to be set for a given number of stampings of any denomination. The setting of the meter must be paid for in advance. One of the advantages of metered mail is that it bypasses the cancellation operation and thereby facilitates handling by the post office. Mail metering also makes the pilfering of stamps impossible, but does not prevent the passage of personal mail in company envelopes through the meters unless there is established a rigid control or censorship over outgoing mail.

1. According to this statement, the postmaster   1.____

    A. is responsible for training new clerks in the use of mail metering machines
    B. usually recommends that both large and small firms adopt the use of mail metering machines
    C. is responsible for setting the meter to print a fixed number of stampings
    D. examines the mail metering machine to see that they are properly installed in the mailroom

2. According to this statement, the use of mail metering machines   2.____

    A. requires the employment of more clerks in a mailroom than does the use of postage stamps
    B. interferes with the handling of large quantities of outgoing mail
    C. does not prevent employees from sending their personal letters at company expense
    D. usually involves smaller expenditures for mailroom equipment than does the use of postage stamps

3. On the basis of this statement, it is MOST accurate to state that   3.____

    A. mail metering machines are often used for opening envelopes
    B. postage stamps are generally used when bulky packages are to be mailed
    C. the use of metered mail tends to interfere with rapid mail handling by the post office
    D. mail metering machines can seal and count letters at the same time

Questions 4-5.

DIRECTIONS: Questions 4 and 5 are to be answered SOLELY on the basis of the following statement.

Forms are printed sheets of paper on which information is to be entered. While what is printed on the form is most important, the kind of paper used in making the form is also important. The kind of paper should be selected with regard to the use to which the form will be subjected. Printing a form on an unnecessarily expensive grade of papers is wasteful. On the other hand, using too cheap or flimsy a form can materially interfere with satisfactory performance of the work the form is being planned to do. Thus, a form printed on both sides normally requires a heavier paper than a form printed only on one side. Forms to be used as permanent records, or which are expected to have a very long life in files, requires a quality of paper which will not disintegrate or discolor with age. A form which will go through a great deal of handling requires a strong, tough paper, while thinness is a necessary qualification where the making of several copies of a form will be required.

4. According to this statement, the type of paper used for making forms   4.____

    A. should be chosen in accordance with the use to which the form will be put
    B. should be chosen before the type of printing to be used has been decided upon
    C. is as important as the information which is printed on it
    D. should be strong enough to be used for any purpose

5. According to this statement, forms that are   5.____

    A. printed on both sides are usually economical and desirable
    B. to be filed permanently should not deteriorate as time goes on
    C. expected to last for a long time should be handled carefully
    D. to be filed should not be printed on inexpensive paper

Questions 6-8.

DIRECTIONS: Questions 6 through 8 are to be answered SOLELY on the basis of the following paragraph.

The increase in the number of public documents in the last two centuries closely matches the increase in population in the United States. The great number of public documents has become a serious threat to their usefulness. It is necessary to have programs which will reduce the number of public documents that are kept and which will, at the same time, assure keeping those that have value. Such programs need a great deal of thought to have any success.

6. According to the above paragraph, public documents may be LESS useful if   6.____

    A. the files are open to the public
    B. the record room is too small
    C. the copying machine is operated only during normal working hours
    D. too many records are being kept

7. According to the above paragraph, the growth of the population in the United States has matched the growth in the quantity of public documents for a period of MOST NEARLY _____ years.   7._____

    A. 50   B. 100   C. 200   D. 300

8. According to the above paragraph, the increased number of public documents has made it necessary to   8._____

    A. find out which public documents are worth keeping
    B. reduce the great number of public documents by decreasing government services
    C. eliminate the copying of all original public documents
    D. avoid all new copying devices

Questions 9-10.

DIRECTIONS: Questions 9 and 10 are to be answered SOLELY on the basis of the following paragraph.

The work goals of an agency can best be reached if the employees understand and agree with these goals. One way to gain such understanding and agreement is for management to encourage and seriously consider suggestions from employees in the setting of agency goals.

9. On the basis of the above paragraph, the BEST way to achieve the work goals of an agency is to   9._____

    A. make certain that employees work as hard as possible
    B. study the organizational structure of the agency
    C. encourage employees to think seriously about the agency's problems
    D. stimulate employee understanding of the work goals

10. On the basis of the above paragraph, understanding and agreement with agency goals can be gained by   10._____

    A. allowing the employees to set agency goals
    B. reaching agency goals quickly
    C. legislative review of agency operations
    D. employee participation in setting agency goals

Questions 11-13.

DIRECTIONS: Questions 11 through 13 are to be answered SOLELY on the basis of the following paragraph.

In order to organize records properly, it is necessary to start from their very beginning and trace each copy of the record to find out how it is used, how long it is used, and what may finally be done with it. Although several copies of the record are made, one copy should be marked as the copy of record. This is the formal legal copy, held to meet the requirements of the law. The other copies may be retained for brief periods for reference purposes, but these copies should not be kept after their usefulness as reference ends. There is another reason for tracing records through the office and that is to determine how long it takes the copy of record to reach the central file. The copy of record must not be kept longer than necessary by the section of the office which has prepared it, but should be sent to the central file as soon as possible so that it can be available to the various sections of the office. The central file can make the copy of record available to the various sections of the office at an early date only if it arrives at the central file as quickly as possible. Just as soon as its immediate or active service period is ended, the copy of record should be removed from the central file and put into the inactive file in the office to be stored for whatever length of time may be necessary to meet legal requirements, and then destroyed.

11. According to the above paragraph, a reason for tracing records through an office is to

    A. determine how long the central file must keep the records
    B. organize records properly
    C. find out how many copies of each record are required
    D. identify the copy of record

11.____

12. According to the above paragraph, in order for the central file to have the copy of record available as soon as possible for the various sections of the office, it is MOST important that the

    A. copy of record to be sent to the central file meets the requirements of the law
    B. copy of record is not kept in the inactive file too long
    C. section preparing the copy of record does not unduly delay in sending it to the central file
    D. central file does not keep the copy of record beyond its active service period

12.____

13. According to the above paragraph, the length of time a copy of a record is kept in the inactive file of an office depends CHIEFLY on the

    A. requirements of the law
    B. length of time that is required to trace the copy of record through the office
    C. use that is made of the copy of record
    D. length of the period that the copy of record is used for reference purposes

13.____

Questions 14-16.

DIRECTIONS: Questions 14 through 16 are to be answered SOLELY on the basis of the following paragraph.

The office was once considered as nothing more than a focal point of internal and external correspondence. It was capable only of dispatching a few letters upon occasion and of preparing records of little practical value. Under such a concept, the vitality of the office force was impaired. Initiative became stagnant, and the lot of the office worker was not likely to be a happy one. However, under the new concept of office management, the possibilities of waste and mismanagement in office operation are now fully recognized, as are the possibilities for the modern office to assist in the direction and control of business operations. Fortunately, the modern concept of the office as a centralized service-rendering unit is gaining ever greater acceptance in today's complex business world, for without the modern office, the production wheels do not turn and the distribution of goods and services is not possible.

14. According to the above paragraph, the fundamental difference between the old and the new concept of the office is the change in the   14._____

    A. accepted functions of the office
    B. content and the value of the records kept
    C. office methods and systems
    D. vitality and morale of the office force

15. According to the above paragraph, an office operated today under the old concept of the office MOST likely would   15._____

    A. make older workers happy in their jobs
    B. be part of an old thriving business concern
    C. have a passive role in the conduct of a business enterprise
    D. attract workers who do not believe in modern methods

16. Of the following, the MOST important implication of the above paragraph is that a present-day business organization cannot function effectively without the   16._____

    A. use of modern office equipment
    B. participation and cooperation of the office
    C. continued modernization of office procedures
    D. employment of office workers with skill and initiative

Questions 17-20.

DIRECTIONS: Questions 17 through 20 are to be answered SOLELY on the basis of the following paragraph.

A report is frequently ineffective because the person writing it is not fully acquainted with all the necessary details before he actually starts to construct the report. All details pertaining to the subject should be known before the report is started. If the essential facts are not known, they should be investigated. It is wise to have essential facts written down rather than to depend too much on memory, especially if the facts pertain to such matters as amounts, dates, names of persons, or other specific data. When the necessary information has been gathered, the general plan and content of the report should be thought out before the writing is actually begun. A person with little or no experience in writing reports may find that it is wise to make a brief outline. Persons with more experience should not need a written outline, but they should make mental notes of the steps they are to follow. If writing reports without dictation is a regular part of an office worker's duties, he should set aside a certain time during the day when he is least likely to be interrupted. That may be difficult, but in most offices there are certain times in the day when the callers, telephone calls, and other interruptions are not numerous. During those times, it is best to write reports that need undivided concentration. Reports that are written amid a series of interruptions may be poorly done.

17. Before starting to write an effective report, it is necessary to   17._____

    A. memorize all specific information
    B. disregard ambiguous data
    C. know all pertinent information
    D. develop a general plan

18. Reports dealing with complex and difficult material should be 18._____

    A. prepared and written by the supervisor of the unit
    B. written when there is the least chance of interruption
    C. prepared and written as part of regular office routine
    D. outlined and then dictated

19. According to the paragraph, employees with no prior familiarity in writing reports may find it helpful to 19._____

    A. prepare a brief outline
    B. mentally prepare a synopsis of the report's content
    C. have a fellow employee help in writing the report
    D. consult previous reports

20. In writing a report, needed information which is unclear should be 20._____

    A. disregarded   B. memorized
    C. investigated   D. gathered

Questions 21-25.

DIRECTIONS: Questions 21 through 25 are to be answered SOLELY on the basis of the following passage.

Positive discipline minimizes the amount of personal supervision required and aids in the maintenance of standards. When a new employee has been properly introduced and carefully instructed, when he has come to know the supervisor and has confidence in the supervisor's ability to take care of him, when he willingly cooperates with the supervisor, that employee has been under positive discipline and can be put on his own to produce the quantity and quality of work desired. Negative discipline, the fear of transfer to a less desirable location, for example, to a limited extent may restrain certain individuals from overt violation of rules and regulations governing attendance and conduct which in governmental agencies are usually on at least an agency-wide basis. Negative discipline may prompt employees to perform according to certain rules to avoid a penalty such as, for example, docking for tardiness.

21. According to the above passage, it is reasonable to assume that in the area of discipline, the first-line supervisor in a governmental agency has GREATER scope for action in 21._____

    A. *positive* discipline, because negative discipline is largely taken care of by agency rules and regulations
    B. *negative* discipline, because rules and procedures are already fixed and the supervisor can rely on them
    C. *positive* discipline, because the supervisor is in a position to recommend transfers
    D. *negative* discipline, because positive discipline is reserved for people on a higher supervisory level

22. In order to maintain positive discipline of employees under his supervision, it is MOST important for a supervisor to 22._____

    A. assure each employee that he has nothing to worry about
    B. insist at the outset on complete cooperation from employees

C. be sure that each employee is well trained in his job
D. inform new employees of the penalties for not meeting standards

23. According to the above passage, a feature of negative discipline is that it   23._____

    A. may lower employee morale
    B. may restrain employees from disobeying the rules
    C. censures equal treatment of employees
    D. tends to create standards for quality of work

24. A REASONABLE conclusion based on the above passage is that positive discipline ben-   24._____
efits a supervisor because

    A. he can turn over orientation and supervision of a new employee to one of his sub-ordinates
    B. subordinates learn to cooperate with one another when working on an assignment
    C. it is easier to administer
    D. it cuts down, in the long run, on the amount of time the supervisor needs to spend on direct supervision

25. Based on the above passage, it is REASONABLE to assume, that an important differ-   25._____
ence between positive discipline and negative discipline is that positive discipline

    A. is concerned with the quality of work and negative discipline with the quantity of work
    B. leads to a more desirable basis for motivation of the employee
    C. is more likely to be concerned with agency rules and regulations
    D. uses fear while negative discipline uses penalties to prod employees to adequate performance

___

KEY (CORRECT ANSWERS)

1.	C		11.	B
2.	C		12.	C
3.	D		13.	A
4.	A		14.	A
5.	B		15.	C
6.	D		16.	B
7.	C		17.	C
8.	A		18.	B
9.	D		19.	A
10.	D		20.	B

21.	A
22.	C
23.	B
24.	D
25.	B

___

TEST 2

Questions 1-6.

DIRECTIONS: Questions 1 through 6 are to be answered SOLELY on the basis of the following passage.

Inherent in all organized endeavors is the need to resolve the individual differences
involved in conflict. Conflict may be either a positive or negative factor since it may lead to
creativity, innovation and progress on the one hand, or it may result, on the other hand, in a
deterioration or even destruction of the organization. Thus, some forms of conflict are desirable, whereas others are undesirable and ethically wrong.

There are three management strategies which deal with interpersonal conflict. In the
divide-and-rule strategy, management attempts to maintain control by limiting the conflict to
those directly involved and preventing their disagreement from spreading to the larger group.
The *suppression-of-differences strategy* entails ignoring conflicts or pretending they are irrelevant. In the *working-through-differences strategy,* management actively attempts to solve or
resolve intergroup or interpersonal conflicts. Of the three strategies, only the last directly
attacks and has the potential for eliminating the causes of conflict. An essential part of this
strategy, however, is its employment by a committed and relatively mature management
team.

1. According to the above passage, the *divide-and-rule strategy tor* dealing with conflict is   1._____
    the attempt to

    A.   involve other people in the conflict
    B.   restrict the conflict to those participating in it
    C.   divide the conflict into positive and negative factors
    D.   divide the conflict into a number of smaller ones

2. The word *conflict* is used in relation to both positive and negative factors in this passage.   2._____
    Which one of the following words is MOST likely to describe the activity which the word
    conflict, in the sense of the passage, implies?

    A.   Competition   B.   Confusion
    C.   Cooperation   D.   Aggression

3. According to the above passage, which one of the following characteristics is shared by   3._____
    both the *suppression-of-differences strategy* and the *divide-and-rule strategy*?

    A.   Pretending that conflicts are irrelevant
    B.   Preventing conflicts from spreading to the group situation
    C.   Failure to directly attack the causes of conflict
    D.   Actively attempting to resolve interpersonal conflict

4. According to the above passage, the successful resolution of interpersonal conflict   4._____
    requires

    A.   allowing the group to mediate conflicts between two individuals
    B.   division of the conflict into positive and negative factors
    C.   involvement of a committed, mature management team
    D.   ignoring minor conflicts until they threaten the organization

5. Which can be MOST reasonably inferred from the above passage? Conflict between two   5._____
    individuals is LEAST likely to continue when management uses

    A. the *working-through differences strategy*
    B. the *suppression-of differences strategy*
    C. the *divide-and-rule strategy*
    D. a combination of all three strategies

6. According to the above passage, a DESIRABLE result of conflict in an organization is   6._____
    when conflict

    A. exposes production problems in the organization
    B. can be easily ignored by management
    C. results in advancement of more efficient managers
    D. leads to development of new methods

Questions 7-13.

DIRECTIONS: Questions 7 through 13 are to be answered SOLELY on the basis of the pas-
              sage below.

    Modern management places great emphasis on the concept of communication. The
communication process consists of the steps through which an idea or concept passes from
its inception by one person, the sender, until it is acted upon by another person, the receiver.
Through an understanding of these steps and some of the possible barriers that may occur,
more effective communication may be achieved. The first step in the communication process is
ideation by the sender. This is the formation of the intended content of the message he wants
to transmit. In the next step, encoding, the sender organizes his ideas into a series of symbols designed to communicate his message to his intended receiver. He selects suitable
words or phrases that can be understood by the receiver, and he also selects the appropriate
media to be used—for example, memorandum, conference, etc. The third step is transmission
of the encoded message through selected channels in the organizational structure. In the
fourth step, the receiver enters the process by tuning in to receive the message. If the
receiver does not function, however, the message is lost. For example, if the message is oral,
the receiver must be a good listener. The fifth step is decoding of the message by the
receiver, as for example, by changing words into ideas. At this step, the decoded message
may not be the same idea that the sender originally encoded because the sender and
receiver have different perceptions regarding the meaning of certain words. Finally, the
receiver acts or responds. He may file the information, ask for more information, or take other
action. There can be no assurance, however, that communication has taken place unless
there is some type of feedback to the sender in the form of an acknowledgement that the
message was received.

7. According to the above passage, *ideation* is the process by which the   7._____

    A. sender develops the intended content of the message
    B. sender organizes his ideas into a series of symbols
    C. receiver tunes in to receive the message
    D. receiver decodes the message

8. In the last sentence of the passage, the word *feedback* refers to the process by which the sender is assured that the   8.____

   A. receiver filed the information
   B. receiver's perception is the same as his own
   C. message was received
   D. message was properly interpreted

9. Which one of the following BEST shows the order of the steps in the communication process as described in the passage?   9.____

   A. 1 - ideation   2 - encoding
      3 - decoding   4 - transmission
      5 - receiving   6 - action
      7 - feedback to the sender

   B. 1 - ideation   2 - encoding
      3 - transmission   4 - decoding
      5 - receiving   6 - action
      7 - feedback to the sender

   C. 1 - ideation   2 - decoding
      3 - transmission   4 - receiving
      5 - encoding   6 - action
      7 - feedback to the   sender

   D. 1 - ideation   2 - encoding
      3 - transmission   4 - receiving
      5 - decoding   6 - action
      7 - feedback to the sender

10. Which one of the following BEST expresses the main theme of the passage?   10.____

   A. Different individuals have the same perceptions regarding the meaning of words.
   B. An understanding of the steps in the communication process may achieve better communication.
   C. Receivers play a passive role in the communication process.
   D. Senders should not communicate with receivers who transmit feedback.

11. The above passage implies that a receiver does NOT function properly when he   11.____

   A. transmits feedback   B. files the information
   C. is a poor listener   D. asks for more information

12. Which one of the following, according to the above passage, is included in the SECOND step of the communication process?   12.____

   A. Selecting the appropriate media to be used in transmission
   B. Formulation of the intended content of the message
   C. Using appropriate media to respond to the receiver's feedback
   D. Transmitting the message through selected channels in the organization

13. The above passage implies that the *decoding process* is MOST NEARLY the reverse of the _____ process.   13.____

   A. transmission   B. receiving
   C. feedback   D. encoding

Questions 14-19.

DIRECTIONS: Questions 14 through 19 are to be answered SOLELY on the basis of the following passage.

It is often said that no system will work if the people who carry it out do not want it to work. In too many cases, a departmental reorganization that seemed technically sound and economically practical has proved to be a failure because the planners neglected to take the human factor into account. The truth is that employees are likely to feel threatened when they learn that a major change is in the wind. It does not matter whether or not the change actually poses a threat to an employee; the fact that he believes it does or fears it might is enough to make him feel insecure. Among the dangers he fears, the foremost is the possibility that his job may cease to exist and that he may be laid off or shunted into a less skilled position at lower pay. Even if he knows that his own job category is secure, however, he is likely to fear losing some of the important intangible advantages of his present position—for instance, he may fear that he will be separated from his present companions and thrust in with a group of strangers, or that he will find himself in a lower position on the organizational ladder if a new position is created above his.

It is important that management recognize these natural fears and take them into account in planning any kind of major change. While there is no cut-and-dried formula for preventing employee resistance, there are several steps that can be taken to reduce employees' fears and gain their cooperation. First, unwarranted fears can be dispelled if employees are kept informed of the planning from the start and if they know exactly what to expect. Next, assurance on matters such as retraining, transfers, and placement help should be given as soon as it is clear what direction the reorganization will take. Finally, employees' participation in the planning should be actively sought. There is a great psychological difference between feeling that a change is being forced upon one from the outside, and feeling that one is an insider who is helping to bring about a change.

14. According to the above passage, employees who are not in real danger of losing their jobs because of a proposed reorganization

    A.   will be eager to assist in the reorganization
    B.   will pay little attention to the reorganization
    C.   should not be taken into account in planning the reorganization
    D.   are nonetheless likely to feel threatened by the reorganization

14.____

15. The passage mentions the *intangible advantages* of a position.
Which of the following BEST describes the kind of advantages alluded to in the passage?

    A.   Benefits such as paid holidays and vacations
    B.   Satisfaction of human needs for things like friendship and status
    C.   Qualities such as leadership and responsibility
    D.   A work environment that meets satisfactory standards of health and safety

15.____

16. According to the passage, an employee's fear that a reorganization may separate him from his present companions is a (n)

    A.   childish and immature reaction to change
    B.   unrealistic feeling since this is not going to happen

16.____

C. possible reaction that the planners should be aware of
D. incentive to employees to participate in the planning

17. On the basis of the above passage, it would be DESIRABLE, when planning a department-mental reorganization, to

    A. be governed by employee feelings and attitudes
    B. give some employees lower positions
    C. keep employees informed
    D. lay off those who are less skilled

17.___

18. What does the passage say can be done to help gain employees' cooperation in a reorganization?

    A. Making sure that the change is technically sound, that it is economically practical, and that the human factor is taken into account
    B. Keeping employees fully informed, offering help in fitting them into new positions, and seeking their participation in the planning
    C. Assuring employees that they will not be laid off, that they will not be reassigned to a group of strangers, and that no new positions will be created on the organization ladder
    D. Reducing employees' fears, arranging a retraining program, and providing for transfers

18.___

19. Which of the following suggested titles would be MOST appropriate for this passage?

    A. PLANNING A DEPARTMENTAL REORGANIZATION
    B. WHY EMPLOYEES ARE AFRAID
    C. LOOKING AHEAD TO THE FUTURE
    D. PLANNING FOR CHANGE: THE HUMAN FACTOR

19.___

Questions 20-22.

DIRECTIONS: Questions 20 through 22 are to be answered SOLELY on the basis of the following passage.

The achievement of good human relations is essential if a business office is to produce at top efficiency and is to be a pleasant place in which to work. All office workers plan an important role in handling problems in human relations. They should, therefore, strive to acquire the understanding, tactfulness, and awareness necessary to deal effectively with actual office situations involving co-workers on all levels. Only in this way can they truly become responsible, interested, cooperative, and helpful members of the staff.

20. The selection implies that the MOST important value of good human relations in an office is to develop

    A. efficiency   B. cooperativeness
    C. tact   D. pleasantness and efficiency

20.___

21. Office workers should acquire understanding in dealing with

    A. co-workers   B. subordinates
    C. superiors   D. all members of the staff

21.___

22. The selection indicates that a highly competent secretary who is also very argumentative   22.____
is meeting office requirements

    A. wholly   B. partly
    C. slightly   D. not at all

Questions 23-25.

DIRECTIONS: Questions 23 through 25 are to be answered SOLELY on the basis of the following passage.

It is common knowledge that ability to do a particular job and performance on the job do
not always go hand in hand. Persons with great potential abilities sometimes fall down on the
job because of laziness or lack of interest in the job, while persons with mediocre talents have
often achieved excellent results through their industry and their loyalty to the interests of their
employers. It is clear; therefore, that in a balanced personnel program, measures of
employee ability need to be supplemented by measures of employee performance, for the
final test of any employee is his performance on the job.

23. The MOST accurate of the following statements, on the basis of the above paragraph, is   23.____
that

    A. employees who lack ability are usually not industrious
    B. an employee's attitudes are more important than his abilities
    C. mediocre employees who are interested in their work are preferable to employees
       who possess great ability
    D. superior capacity for performance should be supplemented with proper attitudes

24. On the basis of the above paragraph, the employee of most value to his employer is NOT   24.____
necessarily the one who

    A. best understands the significance of his duties
    B. achieves excellent results
    C. possesses the greatest talents
    D. produces the greatest amount of work

25. According to the above paragraph, an employee's efficiency is BEST determined by an   25.____

    A. appraisal of his interest in his work
    B. evaluation of the work performed by him
    C. appraisal of his loyalty to his employer
    D. evaluation of his potential ability to perform his work

KEY (CORRECT ANSWERS)

1.	B	11.	C
2.	A	12.	A
3.	C	13.	D
4.	C	14.	D
5.	A	15.	B
6.	D	16.	C
7.	A	17.	C
8.	C	18.	B
9.	D	19.	D
10.	B	20.	D

21.	D
22.	B
23.	D
24.	C
25.	B

TEST 3

DIRECTIONS: Questions 1 through 8 are to be answered SOLELY on the basis of the following information and directions.

Assume that you are a clerk in a city agency. Your supervisor has asked you to classify each of the accidents that happened to employees in the agency into the following five categories:

A. An accident that occurred in the period from January through June, between 9 A.M. and 12 Noon, that was the result of carelessness on the part of the injured employee, that caused the employee to lose less than seven working hours, that happened to an employee who was 40 years of age or over, and who was employed in the agency for less than three years;

B. An accident that occurred in the period from July through December, after 1 P.M., that was the result of unsafe conditions, that caused the injured employee to lose less than seven working hours, that happened to an employee who was 40 years of age or over, and who was employed in the agency for three years or more;

C. An accident that occurred in the period from January through June, after 1 P.M., that was the result of carelessness on the part of the injured employee, that caused the injured employee to lose seven or more working hours, that happened to an employee who was less than 40 years old, and who was employed in the agency for three years or more;

D. An accident that occurred in the period from July through December, between 9 A.M. and 12 Noon, that was the result of unsafe conditions, that caused the injured employee to lose seven or more working hours, that happened to an employee who was less than 40 years old, and who was employed in the agency for less than three years;

E. Accidents that cannot be classified in any of the foregoing groups. NOTE: In classifying these accidents, an employee's age and length of service are computed as of the date of accident. In all cases, it is to be assumed that each employee has been employed continuously in city service, and that each employee works seven hours a day, from 9 A.M. to 5 P.M., with lunch from 12 Noon to 1 P.M. In each question, consider only the information which will assist you in classifying the accident. Any information which is of no assistance in classifying an accident should not be considered.

1. The unsafe condition of the stairs in the building caused Miss Perkins to have an accident on October 14, 2003 at 4 P.M. When she returned to work the following day at 1 P.M., Miss Perkins said that the accident was the first one that had occurred to her in her ten years of employment with the agency. She was born on April 27, 1962.   1.____

2. On the day after she completed her six-month probationary period of employment with the agency, Miss Green, who had been considered a careful worker by her supervisor, injured her left foot in an accident caused by her own carelessness. She went home immediately after the accident, which occurred at 10 A.M., March 19, 2004, but returned to work at the regular time on the following morning. Miss Green was born July 12, 1963 in New York City.   2.____

3. The unsafe condition of a duplicating machine caused Mr. Martin to injure himself in an accident on September 8, 2006 at 2 P.M. As a result of the accident, he was unable to work the remainder of the day, but returned to his office ready for work on the following morning. Mr. Martin, who has been working for the agency since April 1, 2003, was born in St. Louis on February 1, 1968.

3.___

4. Mr. Smith was hospitalized for two weeks because of a back injury resulted from an accident on the morning of November 16, 2006. Investigation of the accident revealed that it was caused by the unsafe condition of the floor on which Mr. Smith had been walking. Mr. Smith, who is an accountant, has been an employee of the agency since March 1, 2004, and was born in Ohio on June 10, 1968.

4.___

5. Mr. Allen cut his right hand because he was careless in operating a multilith machine. Mr. Allen, who was 33 years old when the accident took place, has been employed by the agency since August 17, 1992. The accident, which occurred on January 26, 2006, at 2 P.M., caused Mr. Allen to be absent from work for the rest of the day. He was able to return to work the next morning.

5.___

6. Mr. Rand, who is a college graduate, was born on December, 28, 1967, and has been working for the agency since January 7, 2002. On Monday, April 25, 2005, at 2 P.M., his carelessness in operating a duplicating machine caused him to have an accident and to be sent home from work immediately. Fortunately, he was able to return to work at his regular time on the following Wednesday.

6.___

7. Because he was careless in running down a flight of stairs, Mr. Brown fell, bruising his right hand. Although the accident occurred shortly after he arrived for work on the morning of May 22, 2006, he was unable to resume work until 3 P.M. that day. Mr. Brown was born on August 15, 1955, and began working for the agency on September 12, 2003, as a clerk, at a salary of $22,750 per annum.

7.___

8. On December 5, 2005, four weeks after he had begun working for the agency, the unsafe condition of an automatic stapling machine caused Mr. Thomas to injure himself in an accident. Mr. Thomas, who was born on May 19,1975, lost three working days because of the accident, which occurred at 11:45 A.M.

8.___

Questions 9-10.

DIRECTIONS: Questions 9 and 10 are to be answered SOLELY on the basis of the following paragraph.

An impending reorganization within an agency will mean loss by transfer of several professional staff members from the personnel division. The division chief is asked to designate the persons to be transferred. After reviewing the implications of this reduction of staff with his assistant, the division chief discusses the matter at a staff meeting. He adopts the recommendations of several staff members to have volunteers make up the required reduction.

9. The decision to permit personnel to volunteer for transfer is 9._____

    A. *poor;* it is not likely that the members of a division are of equal value to the division chief

    B. *good;* dissatisfied members will probably be more productive elsewhere

    C. *poor;* the division chief has abdicated his responsibility to carry out the order given to him

    D. *good;* morale among remaining staff is likely to improve in a more cohesive framework

10. Suppose that one of the volunteers is a recently appointed employee who has completed his probationary period acceptably, but whose attitude toward division operations and agency administration tends to be rather negative and sometimes even abrasive. Because of his lack of commitment to the division, his transfer is recommended. If the transfer is approved, the division chief should, prior to the transfer, 10._____

    A. discuss with the staff the importance of commitment to the work of the agency and its relationship with job satisfaction

    B. refrain from any discussion of attitude with the employee

    C. discuss with the employee his concern about the employee's attitude

    D. avoid mention of attitude in the evaluation appraisal prepared for the receiving division chief

Questions 11-16.

DIRECTIONS: Questions 11 through 16 are to be answered SOLELY on the basis of the following paragraph.

Methods of administration of office activities, much of which consists of providing information and *know-how* needed to coordinate both activities within that particular office and other offices, have been among the last to come under the spotlight of management analysis. Progress has been rapid during the past decade, however, and is now accelerating at such a pace that an *information revolution* in office management appears to be in the making. Although triggered by technological breakthroughs in electronic computers and other giant steps in mechanization, this information revolution must be attributed to underlying forces, such as the increased complexity of both governmental and private enterprise, and ever-keener competition. Size, diversification, specialization of function, and decentralization are among the forces which make coordination of activities both more imperative and more difficult. Increased competition, both domestic and international, leaves little margin for error in managerial decisions. Several developments during recent years indicate an evolving pattern. In 1960, the American Management Association expanded the scope of its activities and changed the name of its Office Management Division to Administrative Services Division. Also in 1960, the magazine *Office Management* merged with the magazine *American Business,* and this new publication was named *Administrative Management.*

11.   A REASONABLE inference that can be made from the information in the above para-   11.___
      graph is that an important role of the office manager today is to

      A.   work toward specialization of functions performed by his subordinates
      B.   inform and train subordinates regarding any new developments in computer tech-
           nology and mechanization
      C.   assist the professional management analysts with the management analysis work
           in the organization
      D.   supply information that can be used to help coordinate and manage the other
           activities of the organization

12.   An IMPORTANT reason for the *information revolution* that has been taking place in office   12.___
      management is the

      A.   advance made in management analysis in the past decade
      B.   technological breakthrough in electronic computers and mechanization
      C.   more competitive and complicated nature of private business and government
      D.   increased efficiency of office management techniques in the past ten years

13.   According to the above paragraph, specialization of function in an organization is MOST   13.___
      likely to result in

      A.   the elimination of errors in managerial decisions
      B.   greater need to coordinate activities
      C.   more competition with other organizations, both domestic and international
      D.   a need for office managers with greater flexibility

14.   The word *evolving,* as used in the third from last sentence in the above paragraph,   14.___
      means MOST NEARLY

      A.   developing by gradual changes
      B.   passing on to others
      C.   occurring periodically
      D.   breaking up into separate, constituent parts

15.   Of the following, the MOST reasonable implication of the changes in names mentioned in   15.___
      the last part of the above paragraph is that these groups are attempting to

      A.   professionalize the field of office management and the title of Office Manager
      B.   combine two publications into one because of the increased costs of labor and
           materials
      C.   adjust to the fact that the field of office management is broadening
      D.   appeal to the top managerial people rather than the office management people in
           business and government

16.   According to the above paragraph, intense competition among domestic and interna-   16.___
      tional enterprises makes it MOST important for an organization's managerial staff to

      A.   coordinate and administer office activities with other activities in the organization
      B.   make as few errors in decision-making as possible
      C.   concentrate on decentralization and reduction of size of the individual divisions of
           the organization
      D.   restrict decision-making only to top management officials

Questions 17-21.

DIRECTIONS: Questions 17 through 21 are to be answered SOLELY on the basis of the following passage.

For some office workers, it is useful to be familiar with the four main classes of domestic mail; for others, it is essential. Each class has a different rate of postage, and some have requirements concerning wrapping, sealing, or special information to be placed on the package. First class mail, the class which may not be opened for postal inspection, includes letters, postcards, business reply cards, and other kinds of written matter. There are different rates for some of the kinds of cards which can be sent by first class mail. The maximum weight for an item sent by first class mail is 70 pounds. An item which is not letter size should be marked *First Class* on all sides. Although office workers most often come into contact with first class mail, they may find it helpful to know something about the other classes. Second class mail is generally used for mailing newspapers and magazines. Publishers of these articles must meet certain U.S. Postal Service requirements in order to obtain a permit to use second class mailing rates. Third class mail, which must weigh less than 1 pound, includes printed materials and merchandise parcels. There are two rate structures for this class - a single piece rate and a bulk rate. Fourth class mail, also known as parcel post, includes packages weighing from one to 40 pounds. For more information about these classes of mail and the actual mailing rates, contact your local post office.

17. According to this passage, first class mail is the *only* class which   17.____

    A.   has a limit on the maximum weight of an item
    B.   has different rates for items within the class
    C.   may not be opened for postal inspection
    D.   should be used by office workers

18. According to this passage, the one of the following items which may CORRECTLY be   18.____
    sent by fourth class mail is a

    A.   magazine weighing one-half pound
    B.   package weighing one-half pound
    C.   package weighing two pounds
    D.   postcard

19. According to this passage, there are different postage rates for   19.____

    A.   a newspaper sent by second class mail and a magazine sent by second class mail
    B.   each of the classes of mail
    C.   each pound of fourth class mail
    D.   printed material sent by third class mail and merchandise parcels sent by third
        class mail

20. In order to send a newspaper by second class mail, a publisher MUST   20.____

    A.   have met certain postal requirements and obtained a permit
    B.   indicate whether he wants to use the single piece or the bulk rate
    C.   make certain that the newspaper weighs less than one pound
    D.   mark the newspaper *Second Class* on the top and bottom of the wrapper

21. Of the following types of information, the one which is NOT mentioned in the passage is   21.____
the

    A. class of mail to which parcel post belongs
    B. kinds of items which can be sent by each class of mail
    C. maximum weight for an item sent by fourth class mail
    D. postage rate for each of the four classes of mail

Questions 22-25.

DIRECTIONS: Questions 22 through 25 are to be answered SOLELY on the basis of the following paragraph.

A standard comprises characteristics attached to an aspect of a process or product by which it can be evaluated. Standardization is the development and adoption of standards. When they are formulated, standards are not usually the product of a single person, but represent the thoughts and ideas of a group, leavened with the knowledge and information which are currently available. Standards which do not meet certain basic requirements become a hindrance rather than an aid to progress. Standards must not only be correct, accurate, and precise in requiring no more and no less than what is needed for satisfactory results, but they must also be workable in the sense that their usefulness is not nullified by external conditions. Standards should also be acceptable to the people who use them. If they are not acceptable, they cannot be considered to be satisfactory, although they may possess all the other essential characteristics.

22. According to the above paragraph, a processing standard that requires the use of materials that cannot be procured is MOST likely to be   22.____

    A. incomplete   B. unworkable
    C. inaccurate   D. unacceptable

23. According to the above paragraph, the construction of standards to which the performance of job duties should conform is MOST often   23.____

    A. the work of the people responsible for seeing that the duties are properly performed
    B. accomplished by the person who is best informed about the functions involved
    C. the responsibility of the people who are to apply them
    D. attributable to the efforts of various informed persons

24. According to the above paragraph, when standards call for finer tolerances than those essential to the conduct of successful production operations, the effect of the standards on the improvement of production operations is   24.____

    A. negative   B. negligible
    C. nullified   D. beneficial

25. The one of the following which is the MOST suitable title for the above paragraph is   25.____

    A. THE EVALUATION OF FORMULATED STANDARDS
    B. THE ATTRIBUTES OF SATISFACTORY STANDARDS
    C. THE ADOPTION OF ACCEPTABLE STANDARDS
    D. THE USE OF PROCESS OR PRODUCT STANDARDS

KEY (CORRECT ANSWERS)

1.	B		11.	D
2.	A		12.	C
3.	E		13.	B
4.	D		14.	A
5.	E		15.	C
6.	C		16.	B
7.	A		17.	C
8.	D		18.	C
9.	A		19.	B
10.	C		20.	A

21.	D
22.	C
23.	D
24.	A
25.	B

———————

SUGGESTIONS TO SUPERVISORS FOR THE EFFECTIVE UTILIZATION OF STENOGRAPHERS AND TYPISTS

CONTENTS

SUGGESTIONS TO SUPERVISORS FOR THE EFFECTIVE UTILIZATION OF STENOGRAPHERS AND TYPISTS

Better utilization of stenographic and typing skills cannot be brought about by administrative orders. The need for it can be re-evalued, but it cannot be accomplished by an agency survey. The only way in which maximum use of each employee can be effected is through you who supervise stenographers and typists. You alone can make certain that these employees are using their skills every hour of the day on essential work. You alone can help them to make their maximum contribution to the agency's work program.

I. 8-POINT PROGRAM

Some practical suggestions to help you make more and better use of the skills of your stenographic and typing personnel.

1. CONSERVE ENERGY
   Place desks where there is plenty of light.
   Adjust chairs so that typists' feet rest firmly on the floor.
   Adjust computer tables so that the base of the computer is 12" above the chair seat.
   Locate supplies and equipment within easy reach.
   Provide copyholders or rests to prevent eye strain.
   Keep equipment in good working condition.
   See that typists understand computers and use the tricks of the trade.

2. CONSERVE TIME
   Keep reports, memoranda, and letters short and concise.
   Keep copy requirements as low as possible.
   Make all changes in a rough draft the first time.
   Indicate minor corrections on a final draft in such a way that they can be erased.
   Make corrections in longhand on informal material.
   Use available dictating machines.
   Do not waste time dictating material which is already printed or readily available for copying.
   Provide desk dictionaries or work books for spelling and hyphenation.

3. SIMPLIFY PROCEDURES
   Use form letters and form paragraphs wherever possible.
   Standardize letter salutations and closings.
   Use block formation and open punctuation.
   Use window envelopes
   Write short, informal notes in longhand.

4. USE SKILLS TO ADVANTAGE
   Relieve stenographers and typists of jobs that can be done by messengers or clerks.
   Assign copy work to typists rather than stenographers.
   Dictate to a typist while she types, if a stenographer is not available.
   Tell your personnel office about employees with skills that are not being utilized.

5. **EXPLAIN THE WORK**
See that each typist and stenographer understands:
How the work is to be done.
Why the work is important.
What equipment and materials are to be used.
What standards of quality and quantity are expected.
What her responsibilities are.
Whom she is responsible to.
Where she should go for help.

6. **KEEP SKILLS IN LINE WITH THOSE REQUIRED BY THE JOB**
Place in training stenographers and typists whose skills are below job requirements.
Train no longer than necessary for successful performance.

7. **DICTATE EFFECTIVELY**
Prevent unnecessary interruptions. Have complete information at hand. Speak distinctly.
Spell unusual words and proper names.
Regulate your dictation speed to the stenographer's writing speed
Make yourself responsible for grammar and sentence structure.
Tell the stenographer
How many copies you want.
How you want them set up.
Which material is to be rushed.
Which material is to be in rough draft.
Encourage questions.

8. **COOPERATE WITH OTHERS**
Cooperate in arrangements for pooling stenographic and typing services.
Make two-way arrangements with other supervisors to handle extra work during peak loads.
Report surplus employees to your personnel office immediately.

II. CASE STUDIES

Some studies of utilization problems with which agencies have been faced and the solutions they have developed.

1. MATCHING JOBS AND SKILLS

The Problem
Can a system be worked out for assigning jobs of varying degrees of difficulty to typists with different degrees of skill?

The central office of an important agency had 40 employees doing typing jobs. Their skills ranged from 15 to 80 words a minute. Highly skilled typists were frequently assigned jobs requiring little speed, such as typing cards and labels or filling in forms. On the other hand, slow typists were often given work such as volume copying, where high speed is desirable. The problem was to increase the output of the typists by assigning fast work to fast operators and by training those whose skills did not meet the requirements of their work.

<u>How It Was Solved</u>

The agency made a study of its various typing tasks to determine the skill requirements for each type of work. Eight different kinds of work were listed, and the minimum words per minute for assignment to each type of work was established as follows:

Job	Minimum Words Per Minute for Assignment
Cards and folders	24
Forms and paragraph writing	24
Copy from rough draft	30
Machine dictation	30
Volume copy	40
Statistical tables	*

*Special Requirement: Must have dexterity on number keys

When the various tasks had been rated, each section chief was requested to check the typing skill level of his typists through conference with immediate supervisors and to recommend training for those whose skill was below the minimum necessary for assignment. It was also requested that typists with skills above their job requirements be reassigned to more difficult work, and that new typists be rated as they came on duty and assigned accordingly.

<u>Comment</u>

This program was proposed as an aid to supervisors in carrying out their responsibility for economical use of available typists. Such a program in its initial stages is a morale booster, and more work should result because each typist is being assigned work consistent with her ability for satisfactory performance. Other by-products of the plan are apparent:

    a. It assists in the establishment of realistic training which is based upon work requirements.

    b. It provides a basis for evaluating work and setting standards.

2.   USING FORM LETTERS

<u>The Problem</u>

How can form letters be used to eliminate dictation and typing?

A regional office of a Federal agency received 2,500 documents annually from State agencies within the region and acknowledged each one by letter. Moreover, as each report was forwarded to Washington, a memorandum of transmittal was prepared to accompany it. Both the letter of acknowledgment and the memorandum were routine, but their preparation involved considerable typing and special handling. A study of the problem showed that some kind of acknowledgment was necessary. The same was found to be true of the transmittal memorandum. The problem was how to accomplish the same results without dictating and typing individual letters and memoranda for each document.

How It Was Solved

A form letter, which required but a minimum of typing, was devised to replace the transmittal memorandum. A copy of each form letter was sent to the State agency as notice that the documents had been received by the regional office and forwarded to Washington. The change eliminated entirely the letter to the State agencies and eliminated all but a few lines of typing on the transmittal memorandum to Washington. It was estimated that, as a result of the new method, the regional office would achieve an annual saving of 25,000 lines of typing and the cost of materials and labor involved in the preparation of 2,500 letters. In addition to the saving in costs, the agency would get the job done faster and would not tie up the services of typists on routine tasks.

Comment

This case illustrates the important savings that can be realized by devising forms to replace routine letters and memoranda. Another way to eliminate dictation (if the letters themselves cannot be eliminated) is to devise standard paragraphs which can be incorporated into letters by a typist.

One agency carried the standard-paragraph idea one step further, in correspondence with its field offices, by supplying each field representative with a set of the standard paragraphs. Inquiries were answered by sending the field office the numbers of the appropriate standard paragraphs, thus eliminating the letters of response.

3. POOLING SECRETARIES

The Problem

How can secretaries to individual staff members be organized into a pool to handle all the unit's stenographic and typing work?

In a division of an agency, 12 secretaries were assigned to members of the technical staff. Other members of the staff depended for their dictation and typing work upon a small pool, 2 stenographers and 2 typists, supervised by an administrative assistant.

Because of turnover and the difficult of recruiting new stenographers and typists, the pool had to be discontinued. This left the unit with no facilities available for several members of the staff and with no provisions for handling extra assignments or emergency work.

How It Was Solved

The 12 secretaries were organized into a decentralized pool under the direction of the administrative assistant, to whom staff members sent requests for stenographic and typing assistance. The administrative assistant distributed the assignments of work to the individual secretaries, who continued to handle the work of the staff members to whom they were assigned.

Each secretary was kept busy full time whether her superior was in the office or not. The essential stenographic and typing work of the division and the emergency jobs were handled promptly even though there was no separate pool of stenographers and typists. By virtue of central supervision by the administrative assistant, workloads were evened out among the secretaries, and the efficiency of the unit was increased, with an actual reduction in personnel.

Comment

A variation of this agency's idea is to appoint one of the secretaries as the *head secretary* to receive the requests for services and assign work to the others.

Supervisors who have used the *decentralized pool* arrangement say it will work if the unit chief gives it backing and if the person in charge of the pool is cooperative.

4.   MAKING EXTRA COPIES

Go to copy machine for high volume or computer printer.

5.   RELIEVING SECRETARIES OF FILING

The Problem
      How can secretaries be relieved of the necessity of maintaining the individual office files needed by executives?
      In a section handling a large and increasing volume of correspondence dictated by executives, the secretary of each executive maintained a separate correspondence file. It was recognized that pulling letters from file and filing were duties of which the secretaries might be relieved, but to centralize the office files was not considered a fit move.

How It Was Solved
      The file schemes used by the secretaries were so similar that a relatively simple analysis and the institution of minor changes brought them into conformity. The pulling and filing time was estimated for all the secretaries. Then an adequate number of file clerks were made available to the section and trained, and a schedule was set up.
      The file clerks made a quick round of the offices after each mail delivery to take from file all material indicated to them by the secretaries. They did the filing in a series of visits between and after mail delivery hours. The secretaries were requested not to file at all and to take material from the file only when single items were needed.

Comment
      Under this plan, the secretaries could handle the increased volume of dictation without overtime and without the addition of skilled personnel in the section. Stenographic skill was thus concentrated.

6.   MAKING A SURVEY

The Problem
      How can the stenographic and typing services in an entire section be analyzed and adjusted?
      Faced with the problem of maintaining work loads in spite of recruiting new employees or replacements, a large Federal agency decided upon a survey of the personnel of all its bureaus. Special emphasis was placed on the critical stenographic and typing field. The survey was intended to insure that each position in the various sections was properly defined and classified, that each employee was properly placed, that the sections were not overmanned or undermanned, and that essential work was simplified wherever possible.

How It Was Solved
      Survey teams, made up of a personnel analyst and a methods analyst, worked together to analyze the personnel and the work methods in each section.
      The survey team presented the program first to the division chief and his key supervisors, then to the head of the section, and finally to the employees. From the section head, the team obtained an organization chart for the section, a complete roster of

employees, an office layout chart, copies of all incoming and outgoing forms and correspondence, and production records.

In order to review job classification and personnel placement, the survey team asked each employee to prepare a job description and a personnel qualifications statement showing his education, experience, and special skills. Each employee was also asked to complete a questionnaire, giving his comments on the adequacy of his placement, classification work load, work methods, and working conditions. On occasion, the survey team interviewed individual employees to verify and supplement these statements.

The survey team studied the volume of work done in the section, securing the necessary data from existing records or by counts. A study was also made of how much the average employee produced. The team then determined the total personnel required for an operation by dividing the work volume by the average employee output.

In its survey of work methods, the team looked for opportunities to eliminate steps, simplify procedures, and facilitate operations.

At the conclusion of the survey, the team made a final analysis and prepared an informal report of findings and recommendations on:
- a. Persons who should be assigned more suitable duties
- b. Positions which should be reclassified
- c. Methods of measuring work load
- d. Personnel required to carry the work load
- e. Work methods which could be simplified

These recommendations in a preliminary form were discussed with supervisors; and following this, final recommendations were submitted to the section supervisor. The team then gave the supervisors immediate assistance in putting the approved recommendations into effect.

Comment

This analysis of personnel utilization has resulted in savings in stenographic and typing personnel. For example, in one large bureau with 115 filled stenographic and typing positions, the survey resulted in 36 reassignments and the elimination of 7 positions. Moreover, of 57 unfilled positions, 30 were eliminated.

In a small bureau with 31 filled stenographic and typing positions, there were 3 reassignments and 5 positions were eliminated. Of the 5 vacant positions in this bureau, 2 were eliminated.

Although in this particular case much of the analysis was accomplished by a survey team which made an independent study, the principles involved are applicable by any supervisor who faces a similar problem.

III. SELF-APPRAISAL SHEET FOR THOSE GIVING DICTATION

		Yes	No
1.	Have I a definite period for dictating each day?	_____	_____
2.	Am I allowing the stenographer ample time for transcription before the mail closes?	_____	_____
3.	Am I making every effort to prevent unnecessary interruptions during the dictation period?	_____	_____

		Yes	No
4.	Do I have available all the information that I will require during the dictation period?	_____	_____
5.	Am I concentrating during my dictation so that I do not waste my time and that of the stenographer?	_____	_____
6.	Do I indicate clearly whether material dictated is memorandum, letter, report, or other type of communication?	_____	_____
7.	Do I indicate how many copies I need before the material is typed?	_____	_____
8.	Do I indicate which letters are to be rushed?	_____	_____
9.	Do I ask for a rough draft when I anticipate changes?	_____	_____
10.	Do I make all changes in a rough draft the first time so that the letter must be copied only once?	_____	_____
11.	Do I spell unusual words and proper names and clearly enunciate figures?	_____	_____
12.	Do I enunciate clearly and speak directly to the stenographer?	_____	_____
13.	Am I regulating my dictation speed to the stenographer's writing speed?	_____	_____
14.	Am I giving the stenographer an opportunity to ask questions on points which are not clear to her?	_____	_____
15.	Am I making myself responsible for grammar and sentence structure?	_____	_____
16.	Do I compliment my stenographer when she gets out a nice looking letter or report?	_____	_____
17.	Do I take the blame myself for errors that are my fault?	_____	_____
18.	Do I indicate minor corrections in such a way that the material does not need to be retyped?	_____	_____
19.	Do I make corrections in longhand on informal communications?	_____	_____
20.	Do I avoid keeping my stenographer after office hours to do work that can be done just as well the next day?	_____	_____

IV. SELF-APPRAISAL SHEET FOR SUPERVISORS

		Yes	No
1.	Have I checked to see what percentage of time stenographers and typists are devoting to stenographic and typing work?	_____	_____
2.	Do I assign routine duties not calling for skill in stenography or typing to messengers or clerks?	_____	_____
3.	Do I assign copy work to typists rather than stenographers?	_____	_____
4.	Am I asking for as few copies as possible?	_____	_____
5.	Do I have my typists prepare a master rather than retype many copies?	_____	_____
6.	Have I devised standard paragraphs and form letters whenever I could?	_____	_____
7.	Do I write office messages in longhand or use the telephone rather than dictate memoranda?	_____	_____
8.	Have I reported surplus stenographers and typists or those with more skills than my work requires?	_____	_____
9.	Do I assign work from other units to my stenographers and typists during slack periods?	_____	_____
10.	Am I giving extra help and training to stenographers and typists whose performance is below the standard required on the job?	_____	_____
11.	Does each stenographer and typist have definite instructions about what she is to do and how she is to do it?	_____	_____
12.	Does each stenographer and typist understand why her work is important?	_____	_____
13.	Have I explained to each stenographer and typist what her responsibilities are and to whom she is responsible?	_____	_____
14.	Does each stenographer and typist know where she can go for help?	_____	_____
15.	Have I set standards of quality no higher than the work requires?	_____	_____
16.	Have I reached an agreement with my stenographers and typists on the standards of quantity and quality desired?	_____	_____

		Yes	No
17.	Do I offer constructive criticism to enable them to overcome their faults?	_____	_____
18.	Do I help them to iron out difficulties and dissatisfactions with their work?	_____	_____
19.	Have I checked to see that desks, equipment, and materials are placed in the best possible positions?	_____	_____
20.	Do I supply all available equipment to make the work easier?	_____	_____

CPSIA information can be obtained
at www.ICGtesting.com
Printed in the USA
BVHW011655260620
582395BV00011B/620